Finally Free

Embracing a Life of Abundance & Rest

JAZMIN N. FRANK

© 2021 Jazmin N. Frank

Printed in the United States of America

All rights reserved. No portion of this book may be reproduced, stored in a retrieval system, or transmitted in any form or by any means—electronic, mechanical, photocopy, recording, scanning, or other—without the prior written permission of the publisher. The only exception is brief quotations in printed reviews and certain other noncommercial uses permitted by copyright law.

www.jazminnfrank.com

Cover & interior design by Typewriter Creative Co. Cover photo by René Jordaan Photography on CreativeMarket.com.

Unless otherwise noted, Scripture quotations have been taken from the Christian Standard Bible®, Copyright © 2017 by Holman Bible Publishers. Used by permission. Christian Standard Bible® and CSB® are federally registered trademarks of Holman Bible Publishers.

Scripture quotations marked as from the English Standard Bible are from The ESV® Bible (The Holy Bible, English Standard Version®), copyright © 2001 by Crossway, a publishing ministry of Good News Publishers. Used by permission. All rights reserved.

Some notes taken from the ESV® Study Bible (The Holy Bible, English Standard Version®), copyright ©2008 by Crossway, a publishing ministry of Good News Publishers. Used by permission. All rights reserved.

ISBN 978-1-7364164-1-9 (Paperback)
ISBN 978-1-7364164-2-6 (eBook)

*To the tired, worn out, worn down, and weary.
May you hear Jesus calling you to come lay down
your burdens and rest in His abundant love.
May you find space here to finally live free.*

Table of Contents

	Introduction	7
	Devoted Practices	11
DAY 1:	A Call for Freedom	17
DAY 2:	Seen and Known	23
DAY 3:	Meanwhile in Midian	25
DAY 4:	What Faith Is	31
DAY 5:	When Freedom Feels Impossible	33
DAY 6:	Good News for the Oppressed	39
DAY 7:	Finding Freedom in Rest	41
DAY 8:	Powerful God	49
DAY 9:	The Lord is Great	53
DAY 10:	Hardened Hearts	55
DAY 11:	Search My Heart	61
DAY 12:	A Rhythm of Remembrance	63
DAY 13:	Past Faithfulness, Present Faith	67
DAY 14:	Prepare for Rest	69
DAY 15:	Trusting the Way-Maker	77
DAY 16:	A Way in the Wilderness	81
DAY 17:	The Fullness of Freedom	83
DAY 18:	Look at the Birds	89
DAY 19:	Do Not Test the Lord	91
DAY 20:	Test Your Faith	95
DAY 21:	Surrender to Rest	97

DAY 22:	Consecrated for the Covenant	103
DAY 23:	God's Covenant Love	109
DAY 24:	Love God, Love People	111
DAY 25:	What the Lord Requires	117
DAY 26:	Covenant Celebration	119
DAY 27:	Your Body, His Temple	123
DAY 28:	Riding the Rhythm of Rest	125
DAY 29:	Redemption Story	131
DAY 30:	Light and Salt	137
DAY 31:	A People Set Apart	139
DAY 32:	Chosen People	143
DAY 33:	The God of Justice and Compassion	145
DAY 34:	Trusting the Shepherd	151
DAY 35:	Connect in Community and Enjoy Creation	153
DAY 36:	The God of Grace and Rest	159
DAY 37:	Know that He is God	163
DAY 38:	The Generosity of Forgiveness	165
DAY 39:	Embracing the Gift of Forgiveness	169
DAY 40:	Finally Free	171
DAY 41:	For Freedom We are Free	175
DAY 42	Overflowing from Rest	177

A Note from Jazmin	179
How to Lead a Group Scripture Meditation	181
Sabbath Movement Ideas Chart	185
Notes	193

Introduction

There are a handful of times in my life when I have clearly heard God's voice. It wasn't an audible experience. It felt more like God downloaded words into my heart and mind. And of those experiences, there were two where God said the same six words.

"I want you to be free."

The first time I heard those words, I was in my car. Talking out loud to God is a frequent habit of mine while I'm driving, and on this particular day I was verbally running through all the reasons I should and should not accept a friend's invitation to join her at a writing conference in Nashville. I had recently left my teaching job to pursue writing full-time and this conference seemed like a logical next step down that path. I wanted to go, but there was one big thing holding me back—pursuing a writing career didn't leave me with much wiggle room in my budget.

My gut said I should go to the conference, but my head said I needed to keep a tight rein on my finances. In a huff, I told God, "I just want to be responsible," to which He responded, "I just want you to be free."

The second time I heard those words I was at a church retreat. My heart was pretty raw as I journaled about how messed up I felt, and how confined I was by a long list of expectations I felt from others, myself, and even God. I felt like a failure and that maybe I wasn't as far along in my Christian journey as I thought. After wringing the contents of my heart out onto the page, I paused and felt God speak those same words again.

"I want you to be free."

I've spent so much of my life trying to do the right thing, trying to please God, and love others, sometimes even at the expense of loving myself. I've heard sermons, read books, and listened to teachers who have assured me that Christ came to set us free, but I always had this assumption that freedom was something that was coming and that it was something I had to work hard to achieve. Part of that assumption is true. When Jesus returns, we will experience freedom and abundance like we never have before.

But freedom isn't just a later thing. It's a now thing. And it's not something I have to strive to earn. Freedom is a gift that is meant to be received.

This freedom God gives us goes beyond freeing us from sin and death so. That's a huge piece of it, but it's not the full story of freedom. As we'll explore throughout this study, we are set free to *live* free right here and right now.

We are freed *from* so that we are free *to.*

Over the next six weeks we're going to take a deep dive into the book of Exodus to learn what this great gift of freedom looks like and how we can begin living into it.

Exodus chronicles Israel's release from slavery and their journey into the wilderness where they learn what it means to live freely as God's chosen people. For four hundred years, Israel lived in Egypt as slaves to Pharaoh. During that time, the only thing these generations knew was the sharp end of a whip, the commanding presence of their overseers, and the fact that their lives were not their own. Israel was at the mercy of Egypt's ruler, a man who was driven by fear and a desire for great power. But even in their captivity, Israel cried out to God for release, holding onto the desperate hope that there was more to life than slavery.

Exodus will be our framework for this journey. From God's miraculous rescue in leading Israel out of Egypt to the year spent at the base of Mount Sinai receiving instructions about how their new nation should function, we're going to gain a new understanding of the freedom God gives us. We'll do this by studying Scripture, but also by practicing a few spiritual disciplines, or as I like to call them, devoted practices.

One of the key themes woven throughout the book of Exodus—and one of the keys to living free—is the idea of Sabbath rest. At the end of each week of study, I'm going to invite you to enter into the rhythm of Sabbath. If this concept of a day of rest is new to you, don't worry. In the next section, I'll give you an overview of Sabbath, and each week you'll find a different way to meet with God as you build a regular rhythm of rest into your life.

We're also going to spend a lot of time meditating on Scripture. After each day of study you'll find a day set aside to meditate on God's Word. I'll provide more guidance for how to press into these practices of Sabbath and Scripture meditation in the next section, but I want to encourage you now not to rush these next six weeks.

This study is set up to be handled slowly. We're in no rush here. We're meeting God, we're pressing into freedom, and that, dear heart, takes time. We're not racing to any finish lines. We're here to learn about freedom, rest, and abundance so that we can finally live into the freedom Christ as already given us.

Devoted Practices

If we're not mindful, intentional, and approaching our faith with a heart focused on relationship, it can quickly become all about checking off boxes and getting things done. We can focus more on performance than being present with God. That's why at the beginning of every study, I like to give you a few tools and rhythms to help you treat this time of study less like an assignment to be completed and more like an opportunity to encounter God and grow your relationship with Him. I want these next six weeks to be about connecting with God and your heart on a deeper level. To do that, we're going to focus on three practices that will help us love God, love His story, and live devoted.

PRACTICE #1: STUDY SCRIPTURE WITH INTENTION

Anytime you crack open the Bible, you have the opportunity to get to know God and experience Him through His Word. The Bible is not some antiquated text that has no bearing on our lives today. Every chapter, every verse is relevant because it reveals God's heart, as we'll see in our study of Exodus. Scripture helps us get to know God's character and His story. But more than that, these are His words. When we read the Bible, we enter into conversation with God, and if we enter into this practice intentionally, we'll learn to hear and recognize His voice through Scripture.

For the duration of this study, we're going to focus the majority of our time on the book of Exodus. Each day you will find a passage to read, space to record notes, a brief teaching, and some questions to help you dig deeper into God's Word.

As we spend time in God's Word, here are three simple ways to study Scripture with intention:

1. *Start with prayer.* Since the Bible is God's Word, no one knows what it says better than Him. Invite the Holy Spirit to give you ears to hear and a heart to

understand. Ask Him to teach you about Himself and what this freedom of abundance and rest is that He has for you.

2. *Read with a pen in hand.* I always find it easier to read my Bible with intention when I have a pen in hand to underline verses that stick out to me or to write notes in the margins. I find that when you read with a pen in hand, it becomes less about reading and more about entering into conversation with the Lord.

3. *Take notes.* I've provided a blank space at the beginning of each day of study for you to record your own notes, insights, questions, and connections as you read. Make use of that space. I will provide teaching and my own insights as we move through Exodus, but this study will mean more, and you will glean a lot more, if you are willing to study with the intention of encountering God through His Word for yourself.

PRACTICE #2: MEDITATE ON THE WORD

Another aspect of studying the Bible intentionally is to take time to meditate on a passage. This is something we will practice often throughout the next six weeks.

That word "meditate" can make us feel a little uncomfortable. That's because we often connect it with more Eastern practices of sitting with crossed legs and our thumb and forefinger forming O's as someone chants. That isn't the type of meditation we're talking about here, so you can breathe easy.

To meditate simply means to sit long or think deeply about a particular thought, idea, or passage. It is the same word the Psalmist uses in Psalm 1:2 to describe a righteous person: "his delight is in the Lord's instruction, and he meditates on it day and night."

A note on this verse in the ESV Study Bible describes that word meditate as "an active pondering, perhaps even muttering to oneself in pursuit of insight."[1]

After each day of study, you will have a day to meditate on Scripture. We'll use a Scripture meditation practice called Lectio Divina to guide us.

In a Lectio Divina there are five different movements of the meditation practice. I've adapted the practice found in Ruth Haley Barton's book *Sacred Rhythms*.[2] (Side note: This is a great resource to keep handy if you want to dig even deeper into the practice Lectio Divina and other spiritual disciplines.) Each of these movements will be provided for you on our meditation days, but here is an overview of the flow:

1. Read the Word
2. Meditate on the Word
3. Respond to the Word
4. Rest in the Word
5. Live the Word

If you are interested in leading a Scripture meditation with your small group, you will find a guide in the back of this book that will walk you through that process and help you to prepare.

PRACTICE #3: SABBATH

The practice of Sabbath is a cornerstone of the Jewish faith. It was first introduced in the book of Exodus and is a defining piece of Israel's newfound freedom after leaving Egypt. Sabbath was meant to set Israel apart from the other nations and remind them of God's care and provision, as well as their own humanity and limitations. Under Pharaoh, Israel lived a life of constant work, but in God's kingdom, He calls His people into rest.

If you are unfamiliar with Sabbath, it is one twenty-four hour period where God's people stop their work, take a break, rest, and enjoy being in God's presence. It is a revitalizing practice that invites us to rest in the abundance of God and trust that He will take care of us even when we are not working. Sabbath invites us to give up this constant need to perform, accumulate, and conquer our to-do lists. It is a day of worship, community, connection, and creativity.

My friend Stephanie has been studying and practicing Sabbath intentionally for the last few years and has come to see Sabbath as a series of five movements: Prepare, Surrender, Connect, Enjoy, and Overflow. We'll be exploring these movements more in-depth in the coming weeks and learn how to use them in our own Sabbath practice. You can also find a quick reference guide to these movements in the back of this book, with Scripture passages and ideas about how to engage in each of these five areas.

Don't let this idea of Sabbath overwhelm you. Maybe you're already thinking that you can't do this, that you don't have time to take a day off. You need that paycheck. You need to get the kids to their activities. You need to get those chores done because there is no other time during the week.

I know. I'll be the first to admit that Sabbath isn't easy. It takes work to rest well. It takes preparation and requires us to shift our focus from striving to be more productive to enter into the rhythms of rest God established. It's time for us to stop treating rest as a reward we can indulge in when the work is done. Rather, we should be making rest a priority.

I don't expect you to perfect Sabbath or any of these practices. In fact, perfection shouldn't even be the goal. The point here is to allow God to shape us and grow us through these practices. The only thing I ask is that you show up. Try. Allow these practices to be messy, uncomfortable, and imperfect. Even the seeming imperfections can be places to get to know God and our own hearts.

Blessings on the journey, dear heart. And if you haven't already, think about finding a buddy or gathering a group to work through this study together. It's always easier to study and practice spiritual disciplines in a community, where you have others to whom you are accountable and who are taking this journey with you.

Now, as we begin, let's pray:

> *Father, we're about to embark on a journey. We're going to dig into Your Word and we're going to read the story of how You rescued Israel and brought them into freedom. Give us understanding. Help us see and know and experience this freedom that you have given us, and teach us to live into that freedom. You have set us free so that we can live free, and we are hungry for soul-level freedom. We acknowledge that freedom is what You want for us, so help us press into Your abundance and rest and learn to live free.*

Week One

Day 1: A Call for Freedom

STUDY EXODUS 1-2

It's always difficult beginning a new study. Even if you've read a particular passage or book of Scripture previously—even if you've read it several times—there is a kind of settling in that needs to happen when we approach it.

Bible studies are intentional. We're digging in for a particular purpose, with a goal in mind, and we're reading through a specific lens.

The book of Exodus is a pretty familiar book. It's one a lot of Sunday school lessons are pulled from, and for good reason. Exodus houses one of the most influential experiences in the Jewish faith, and since Christianity finds its roots in Judaism, the words of Exodus feed our faith too.

The first half of the book of Exodus is really exciting and powerful. The plagues, the miracles, the Red Sea—it all makes for a very theatrical and engaging read. But once Israel has crossed the sea and is free, their time camping out at Mount Sinai can almost feel like we're reading an entirely different book.

I don't want us entering into this study half-heartedly, feeling like the stories of Exodus are too familiar, or that the passages about the Law are irrelevant. As with any study, we are reading and studying with a purpose, and that purpose is to encounter the God of freedom in every chapter. That purpose is to learn how to embrace a life of abundance and rest.

No matter how familiar you are with the book of Exodus, I want you to set aside what you know. Let your knowledge and familiarity take a back seat. Approach these chapters with a fresh set of eyes and read through the lens of freedom.

So, as we dive into these opening chapters of Exodus, take a deep breath and let it out slowly. Release any expectations or assumptions you're entering this study with. Ask God to prepare your heart to receive whatever it is He has for you here.

Ready to begin? Great!

The book of Exodus picks up from where Genesis left off. In order to understand the significance of what lies ahead in today's passage and the entirety of Exodus, we need to jump backward in time a bit and take a brief survey of the book of Genesis.

Genesis is the very first book of the Bible. Over the first eleven chapters of Genesis, we find accounts of the stories of Creation, the Fall, the Flood, and the Tower of Babel. Then in Genesis 12, things take a turn. The narrative zooms in on one family through whom God promises to bless every nation. The patriarch of this family is a guy named Abraham (Genesis 12:1-3). When God calls Abraham out of the land of Ur, Abraham is childless, but God promises to bring an entire nation from this one man.

When God makes this covenant with Abraham, the Lord reveals some rather surprising information:

Then the LORD said to Abram, "Know this for certain: Your offspring will be resident aliens for four hundred years in a land that does not belong to them and will be en-

WEEK ONE

slaved and oppressed. However, I will judge the nation they serve, and afterward they will go out with many possessions" (Genesis 15:13-14).

What information does God reveal about Abraham's descendants?

A few generations after God spoke those words to Abraham, Joseph, Abraham's great-grandson, is sold into slavery in Egypt because of his brothers' jealousy. Even in slavery, and later when he is wrongfully imprisoned, Joseph remains faithful to God and experiences God's blessing. Through a series of events (which you can read all about in Genesis 37-41), Joseph is given a position of power and saves Egypt, the surrounding nations, and even his own family from a famine. After realizing that Joseph is alive and well in Egypt, his family makes the move from Canaan to Egypt, and all the past tensions between the brothers and Joseph are forgiven.

At the very end of Genesis we see another bit of foreshadowing of what God is going to accomplish with this family.

Read Genesis 50:24-25. What is revealed here about the future of Israel?

Before Israel even existed, God told Abraham that his descendants would be held in bondage by another nation, but He promised to free them. He even spoke of Abraham's future family leaving the land where they were oppressed with an abundance of wealth. That promise was reaffirmed on Joseph's deathbed, when he assured his brothers and children that they would one day return to the land they left.

It's important to know Israel's history as we turn the page to Exodus 1 and 2. Israel's time in Egypt was something God knew about long before they got there, and He had a plan to lead them out again. Knowing this makes Exodus that much more interesting to me. It isn't just a book about powerful acts of God or His signs and wonders. It is God's plan of salvation for Israel.

Look back at your reading from the first two chapters of Exodus. What do we learn about Israel's situation now?

Before we go any further, we need to feel the weight of Israel's position.

Israel had lived happily in their new home, until their growing family was seen as a threat. As a way to subdue their people, Pharaoh placed Israel under the firm hand of forced labor. Enslaving the Hebrews was an act of fear, control, and self-preservation on Pharaoh's part. He needed to be the one with all the power, the one in control. He needed to be god of his nation and his life.

Unfortunately, Israel was the unhappy recipient of Pharaoh's jealous and fearful wrath. They were enslaved. Their children were taken and thrown into the Nile. And it's likely that the God of their fathers—the God who brought Joseph to Egypt in the first place to save his family—felt silent. Under the burden of slavery, the people surrendered to their new identity as slaves and they lived that way for generations.

Can you feel the hopelessness, the oppression, the numbness, anger, resentment, and longing Israel must have felt? Do you connect with their story in any way?

There is no need for freedom unless one is not free, and Israel was not free. They were held captive by a powerful hand, but eventually, the souls of these slaves woke up enough to remember that they were made for more than this. Israel was not meant to be a family of brick builders, housemaids, and tradesmen bound to their masters.

Israel was made to be free, to flourish, and to fill the land God had promised them.

We share the same identity. We are made to be free.

WEEK ONE

As I reflect on Israel's position, I can't help but think back to the Garden of Eden and that moment when sin entered the world. Humans thrived in the Garden and in relationship with God until Satan made his move, whispered a little lie into Eve's ear, and humanity fell into the bondage of sin. Everything was broken and God was distant. Like Israel, we were no longer free.

We may not have a task master standing over us, whip at the ready if we fail to complete our assigned quota of bricks, but we do face different bondages that hold us captive and keep us from living the abundant life God created us for.

We live in the bondage of fear and anxiety.

We are bound by unhealthy mindsets about work and accomplishment.

We enslave ourselves to the bondage of comparison.

We experience the bondage of spiritual oppression.

We give in to the bondage of the idea of self-sufficiency.

There are things in this world that keep us from living free. There is a very real enemy that, like Pharaoh, would do anything to hold us captive under his tyrannical thumb and keep us from thriving.

But that is not the goodness God created us for. That is not the abundant life He intended us to have. Ever since that bite of fruit was taken, God has been working to get us back and set us free.

Israel's story is another leg of His mission. It is a very real history of a real group of people God sets free, but it is also an image of God's work in our lives. These first two chapters of Exodus help us see that freedom is already on its way—for Israel, and for us.

My favorite portion of today's Scripture reading is Exodus 2:23-25. Up to this point, these first two chapters of Exodus have detailed Israel's horrific situation, but in these few verses, we feel the winds change. Their situation hasn't changed yet, but hope enters in because God hears the cries of His people. He remembers His covenant. He sees the situation Israel is in, and He knows.

He hears.

He remembers.

He sees.

He knows.

Those are the words that describe a God who is about to make a move, and it's going to be even more amazing than Israel could ever imagine. They were crying out for freedom from their bondage, but God was preparing to give them so much more.

In what ways do you feel bound up in your life right now?

Are you ready for God to set you free? Ask Him now to continue His freeing work in your life. Cry out to the God who sees, knows, hears, and remembers.

Day 2: Seen and Known

MEDITATE ON PSALM 139:7-12

In between days of study, we're going to take a day to pause and meditate on a short passage of Scripture. These passages will be related to the Exodus passage we just studied. The goal here is to make space for God to speak and for us to listen.

Today we're going to spend time dwelling on some words from the Psalms that reveal God's intimate knowledge of us and His constant presence. The prompts below will lead you through today's Scripture meditation. Go slow. Take your time. Allow yourself ample space to reflect on and respond to God's Word.

Prepare: Be still before the Lord. Ask Him to prepare your heart to read and engage with this Scripture today. Lay your heart open before Him and ask Him to speak.

Read the Word: Read the passage slowly. What words or phrases stand out to you?

Meditate on the Word: Read the passage again. How does this word or phrase connect to your life?

Respond to the Word: Read the passage again. Be honest with God about your response to this word and passage. How do you feel about it? What are you thinking? How are you responding to God? How is God inviting you to respond?

Rest in the Word: Read the passage one more time. Simply rest in God's Word. Submit yourself to His presence and just be present with Him.

Live the Word: How will you live into what you read and heard today?

Day 3: Meanwhile in Midian

STUDY EXODUS 3-4

"Meanwhile."

I love that this is the word that begins our reading today. It indicates that, while the events in front of us are taking up all of our attention, off to the side and over yonder, something else is happening—something that could affect the current situation.

If you'll remember, Exodus 2 ended with a whisper of hope. Israel, though living as slaves, cried out for relief and freedom. And while their situation hasn't changed, we as readers know that God heard them, and He is about to do something. I don't know about you, but I'm on the edge of my seat with anticipation.

What is God going to do?!

To answer that question, our biblical author redirects our attention to the plains of Midian and a man named Moses. Moses was introduced in Exodus 2. Though we haven't addressed his part in the story yet, he is definitely our focus for today.

Flip back through Exodus 2. What do we know about Moses so far?

When we encounter him in today's reading, Moses has been in the wilderness for forty years, since he fled Egypt after killing an Egyptian taskmaster. Though he had been raised in Pharaoh's palace under the care of Pharaoh's daughter, Moses seems fully content with his new life and his new family in the land of Midian.

He's content, at least until his eye notices a burning bush while going about his shepherding routine. Intrigued by the phenomenon, Moses steps closer and quickly learns that God is present.

What does God ask Moses to do that signifies that this moment is a holy one (verse 5)?

When Moses gets close enough and God begins to speak, the first words He says—after Moses' sandals are removed—establish God's identity.

Who does God identify Himself as (Exodus 3:6)?

By listing off Israel's patriarchs, God establishes Himself as the God of covenant.

A covenant was a binding contract between two people that usually had dire consequences if one party broke contract. God made a covenant with Abraham to bless and multiply his descendants and give his family land. Nothing was required of

Abraham except that he remain faithful to God (Genesis 17:1-2). That covenant was transferred to Abraham's son Isaac (Genesis 26:2-5) and from Isaac to his son Jacob (Genesis 28:13-15).

That covenant was rooted in God's promise to take care of Abraham's family and to bless all the nations through him. Generations later, this covenant saw its complete fulfillment when Jesus, a descendent of Abraham, came to save His people—and the whole world—from their sins (Matthew 1:20-21). Jesus' death on the cross and His resurrection was the ultimate rescue mission. But I'm getting way ahead of myself.

Let's come back to the book of Exodus where we left Moses standing barefoot before the burning bush on the mountain.

The God of the covenant—the God of blessing and care and compassion—called Moses aside from his shepherding job for a very important reason.

Look back at Exodus 3:7-10. What is God's purpose for calling Moses to the bush?

This interaction at the bush reiterates what was already told to us as readers at the end of Exodus 2. God is not unaware of Israel's plight in Egypt. He has a plan to usher them out of slavery and into abundant freedom, and Moses is the one God has chosen to help Him carry out His plan.

How does Moses respond to God's plan?

While the plan sounds amazing, the moment God informs Moses that he is God's front man to lead this campaign, Moses is full of arguments. The rest of today's passage details Moses' desire to reject the call along with his long list of reasons why he isn't the right person. His excuses range from his inability to speak, to his fear that the people won't believe that God sent him. But God meets every one of Moses' arguments with a promise of presence and victory. Moses won't be doing this alone, and the result will be freedom for the people. God also gives Moses physical signs to perform for Pharaoh and Israel if they don't believe that God was the one who sent Moses. God also gives Moses a partner, his Hebrew brother Aaron, who will speak the words God gives Moses.

The promise of Israel's freedom is exciting, but the road ahead isn't going to be easy. In fact, it's about to get messy, but freedom itself is messy. There are obstacles to overcome, oppressors to overthrow, and mindsets of the oppressed that need overridden. While Moses may be hesitant about the job ahead, God is not. He is about to bring freedom to His people, and He has called Moses to be an agent to help make that happen.

The funny thing about Moses is that he is bound up in his own kind of bondage. While he made it out of Egypt years before, fear, regret, and shame all plague him. Now he's headed back into the land he escaped with instructions to lead Israel out. But this journey isn't just for Israel's sake. I believe God calls Moses because He knows this experience will be freeing for Moses too. As confirmation that God's words will come about, He promises to bring Moses back to this very mountain, except when he returns, his people will be free. We'll also find Moses a changed man living in freedom too.

In order to experience that, though, Moses needs to act on faith and return to Egypt. Once he is reunited with his brother, Moses and Aaron approach the Hebrews and share the words God spoke to them about their coming freedom, and it brings the people to worship: "The people believed, and when they heard that the LORD had paid attention to them and that He had seen their misery, they knelt low and worshiped" (Exodus 4:31).

We're not the only ones holding onto hope. The people's hope has been awakened too. Freedom is coming. God is going to do whatever it takes to set His people free.

What is your response to God introducing Himself as the God of covenant promise? How does that encourage or challenge you?

WEEK ONE

Do you believe God sees and hears you? Do you believe that He has a plan for your life? Do you believe He wants you to be free from the things holding you captive? Reflect on those questions and your belief about God.

Day 4: What Faith Is

MEDITATE ON HEBREWS 11:1-3

Though he was hesitant at first, Moses acted in great faith when he returned to Egypt and shared the words of God's plan for freedom with his people and with Pharaoh. In today's Scripture meditation, we're going to settle into the words of Hebrews 11 and explore what faith is. If the journey to freedom requires faith, we should know what God is inviting us into.

Prepare: Be still before the Lord. Ask Him to prepare your heart to read and engage with this Scripture. Lay your heart open before Him and ask Him to speak.

Read the Word: Read the passage slowly. What words or phrases stand out to you?

Meditate on the Word: Read the passage again. How does this word or phrase connect to your life?

Respond to the Word: Read the passage again. Be honest with God about your response to this word and passage. How do you feel about it? What are you thinking? How are you responding to God? How is God inviting you to respond?

Rest in the Word: Read the passage one more time. Simply rest in God's Word. Submit yourself to His presence and just be present with Him.

Live the Word: How will you live into what you read and heard today?

Day 5: When Freedom Feels Impossible

STUDY EXODUS 5-6

Things get worse before they get better. That old cliché has become a reality for Israel. After crying out to the Lord and receiving word from Moses and Aaron that God has heard them and is coming to their aid, Pharaoh's hand comes down hard on the Israelites. Rather than letting the people go, as Moses requested, Pharaoh increases their workload and treats them even more harshly. The people are denied the straw needed for the making of bricks and they are forced to find straw themselves, while still meeting the same quota of bricks.

Why do you think Pharaoh's response to Moses' request for Israel's freedom is to increase their work?

Here's the thing about freedom: Opposition and doubt will always rise up against the promise of freedom. It's why freedom feels so hard to get, and why we protect it so aggressively once we have it. Those things or people that hold us captive are powerful and oppressive, and they are threatened by the desire for freedom. When the hope of freedom rises up, oppressive forces rise up to squelch that hope. Israel experiences this firsthand.

If Pharaoh could exhaust them, they would forget this notion of freedom. If their request for release is met with more work and a heavier burden, they might think twice about pursuing it. And since Israel is under Pharaoh's control, the people lose hope. Rather than pressing forward in the hope of God's deliverance, they succumb to the pressure of Pharaoh's heavy hand.

Maybe like me you wonder why Israel gives up so easily. If God has promised, why don't they hold on to belief? That's an easy question to ask on this side of the story when we know what is coming. We know things that they don't know. We know God will come through. We know Israel will be freed. We know that God will prove Himself more powerful than Pharaoh, but they don't know that. All they have to go on is their own experience, and their experience says that God is far off, Pharaoh is more powerful, and slavery is their identity.

But let's put ourselves in Israel's sandals. By this point, the nation of Israel has been in Egypt for four hundred years and of those centuries in this foreign land, many of those years have been spent in slavery. That means the current generation has no recollection of freedom. All they have ever known is being under someone else's control. All they know is the back-breaking labor of making bricks and fulfilling duties for their Egyptian masters. So when Pharaoh's response to Moses' request to free Israel is more work, the people submit. They lose hope.

They also get angry. They're so upset, in fact, that they turn on Moses and Aaron and call for God's judgment to come down on them because of Pharaoh's response. The people are ready to give up this notion of freedom and send Moses and Aaron packing, but Moses turns back to God.

Look at Exodus 5:22-23. Is there anything about Moses' prayer and interaction with God that surprises you?

WEEK ONE

At this point, Moses is probably remembering the experience at the burning bush, God's call, and His promise to set Israel free. Circumstances, however, are making God's words seem doubtful, and Moses calls Him on it. My friend Stephanie would summarize Moses' words this way: "You said you would rescue these people, so do your job!"

Perhaps that feels intense or irreverent, but God doesn't strike Moses down. He doesn't call him out on his harsh words. Instead, God enters conversation with Moses and responds to his accusations.

Summarize the Lord's response to Moses in Exodus 6:1-13?

God is a promise-keeping God. That is a character trait you can track throughout the entirety of the Bible. Even when humans doubt and question His methods or His seeming lack of movement, God often meets their doubt with a reaffirmation of His promise and His character. Here in Egypt, God reaffirms that He is the God of covenant and He will keep the covenant He made with Israel's forefathers. He also affirms that He has heard the people's affliction and cries for help, and He will save them. God also gives words for Moses to speak to the people, to assure them of His plan. Moses obediently delivers God's message to the people, but the people of Israel aren't so keen on hearing more words from the Lord or from Moses. The way Scripture puts it, the people "did not listen to him because of their broken spirit and hard labor" (Exodus 6:9).

Have you ever had trouble receiving God's Word? What made it so difficult for you?

Though the people lacked belief and even Moses doubted how Pharaoh would listen if his own people would not, their doubt does not keep God from acting. His plan is still to bring about freedom for His people and He is on course to do so. Nothing will dissuade Him. He reaffirms His promise. It's going to happen.

We the readers know that because the author gives us a hint. Toward the end of Exodus 6 we encounter something that feels out of place—a genealogy, the family history of Moses and Aaron.

Genealogies are passages of Scripture that are often difficult to read because they just seem like a long list of names. It can be tempting to skim through or skip those passages altogether. Somewhere along the way, someone taught me not to skim through the repetitive nature of genealogies, but to pay attention to the variations. Generally, these lists follow a particular pattern—so-and-so was the father of so-and-so, who had a son named so-and-so. Within those patterns, however, sometimes the author breaks rhythm and takes a little rabbit trail to tell us more about a particular person or event.

In this genealogy in Exodus 6, we find one of these pattern breaks.

Read Exodus 6:14-25 again. What variations or breaks in the pattern do you notice?

This family record begins with the sons of Reuben, Simeon, and Levi, three of the twelve sons of Jacob. The families of Reuben and Simeon follow a similar pattern, but once we get to Levi, that family line is the focus for the rest of the list.

Why? Because this is the line of Moses and Aaron. The heading of this passage keys us into that fact, but we're also shown this as the author focuses on the two brothers, and specifically Aaron. The interesting thing is that the list doesn't stop with listing Aaron and Moses as the sons of Amram. We see breaks in patterns where Amram, Aaron, and Aaron's son Eleazar take wives, and those wives bear them sons. We're tracing a lineage here, establishing Moses and Aaron's place among the people of Israel. The author is also planting some seeds here, because in a not-too-distant future, God will set aside Moses and Aaron's line—the Levites—as His priesthood. One day Aaron's line will serve the Lord as priests, not in Egypt, but in the land He will lead them to. And in case we're still hesitant about the Israel's future freedom, verses 26-27 are clear. These two men, these sons of the tribe of Levi, are the two the

WEEK ONE

Lord has called to lead Israel out of Egypt.

The Lord who promised will faithfully keep His word.

In what ways do you feel like your freedom is being challenged or squelched?

What truth can you hold on to as you continue to wait for freedom?

Day 6: Good News for the Oppressed

MEDITATE ON ISAIAH 61:1-3

One of the ideas we will keep returning to throughout this study is that, while Israel cried out for physical release from their bondage, the freedom God planned to give them—and us—is much more involved. In today's Scripture meditation, we're going to settle into a short passage that joyfully outlines what this freedom is. This passage is the same one that Jesus reads from when His ministry begins, and He declares Himself the fulfillment of these words.

Prepare: Be still before the Lord. Ask Him to prepare your heart to read and engage with this Scripture. Lay your heart open before Him and ask Him to speak.

Read the Word: Read the passage slowly. What words or phrases stand out to you?

Meditate on the Word: Read the passage again. How does this word or phrase connect to your life?

Respond to the Word: Read the passage again. Be honest with God about your response to this word and passage. How do you feel about it? What are you thinking? How are you responding to God? How is God inviting you to respond?

Rest in the Word: Read the passage one more time. Simply rest in God's Word. Submit yourself to His presence and just be present with Him.

Live the Word: How will you live into what you read and heard today?

Day 7: Finding Freedom in Rest

SABBATH

....

One of the bondages we often experience is the bondage of endless activity and work. Israel experienced that in their slavery in Egypt. Work never ended for them. Even when the hope of freedom was promised, Pharaoh stepped in a made their load even heavier. But that wasn't God's plan for them. Humans weren't made to work themselves to death. They were created to live out of a place of rest and abundance.

Part of the freedom afforded us through Jesus is that we are invited to return to a place of rest—the same kind of rest Adam and Eve experienced in the Garden before sin entered the picture. This is a holistic kind of rest. It is the kind of rest where we physically stop work, we take a break, and we just enjoy being for a while. It is the kind of rest where, instead of continuing in the constant pressure to achieve or get our needs met, we lean into the care and provision of God. We trust Him to do what He said He will do.

Sabbath, you could argue, is the antithesis of slavery that restores our identity as children of God. For Israel, Sabbath was a part of their law, a command they were required to obey. While we as modern believers are not bound by the Old Testament law, there is a reason God placed such a high priority on Sabbath. It is a way of returning to the life He intended for us where we are dependent upon Him and confident in our identity as His children. Sabbath rest is what we are made for. We're wired for it, so let's learn how to enter into it.

For this first week of Sabbath, I want you to make space in your week to stop your work and rest.

Traditionally, Sabbath would occur Friday at sundown to Saturday around the same time. Not every schedule allows for this, but pick a 24 hour period that works for you and set it aside as your Sabbath day. If you live with family or in community, invite them to join you. Write it on your calendar and make the commitment to set aside your work for that one day and enjoy the freedom of resting.

It might not feel restful at the beginning. In fact, the first few Sabbaths may be quite difficult. That's okay. If you're not used to the rhythm of taking a day off, your body, mind, and soul will need time to adjust. It's called a letdown period. During this time, your body learns that it isn't actually wired for endless work and that you can rest and enjoy the freedom of a day off.

As we begin this rhythm of Sabbath, in addition to choosing your Sabbath day, it's also important to establish what Sabbath is and what it is not. Prayerfully making these decisions ahead of time will help you rest better and make space to spend time with God.

The goal is to keep things simple and set some clear boundary lines. There may be weeks when Sabbath doesn't look the way you planned, and there is grace for that. You may also find that as you continue to practice Sabbath there are things from this original plan that will need tweaked and that's okay. Sabbath is a practice. It is meant to be shaped. It is meant to grow with you. The core pieces of Sabbath—a full day off, committing your time to God, and spending time in worship—will remain the same, but how you participate in each of those things will probably look a little different in each new season. Our purpose here, though, is to start forming our Sabbath rhythms.

Use the guided questions below to establish boundaries for your Sabbath. I've included an example of my Sabbath boundaries to give you an idea of what this could look like. Once you've established some boundaries for your Sabbath, set the date and keep it. To give you an extra bit of accountability, I've included a Sabbath reflection. Use this space to reflect on your Sabbath experience and continue to shape your practice with the Lord and your community.

Example:

My Sabbath day will be: Every Friday evening to Saturday evening.

Sabbath will be a day for: Resting, sleeping in, spending time with my family and/ or my community, doing things I enjoy, giving my heart some attention.

Sabbath will not be a day for: Chores, meetings, catching up on work, finishing things on my to-do list, lots of running around, household errands, overthinking how I spend my time, questioning my eating or food choices.

Now it's your turn. Establish your Sabbath day and take time to ask God what this day is for, and what it is not for.

My Sabbath day will be:

Sabbath will be a day for:

Sabbath will not be a day for:

SABBATH REFLECTION

How did Sabbath go for you this week?

How did you intentionally connect with God during Sabbath?

What did you enjoy about Sabbath this week?

Was there anything that kept you from resting well?

How might you better prepare for Sabbath next week?

WEEK ONE

Is there anything from your "Yes" list that you'd like to incorporate in your next Sabbath practice?

Week Two

Day 8: Powerful God

STUDY EXODUS 7-8

Perhaps the opening verses of today's passage feel a bit repetitive to read, as it again details God's promises and His plan for Israel's freedom, but Moses and Aaron needed it.

They had just faced immense opposition, both from Pharaoh and from the Israelites. God had called them to lead the people out of Egypt, but all they saw before them were roadblocks and resistance. Pharaoh was hard-hearted and hard-headed, and the people sank back into their familiar mindset as slaves. Their hope had been dashed, and Moses and Aaron were discouraged too.

In His goodness, God came to Moses and Aaron and assured them of His plan. Yes, Israel would go free, but not without a fight. Pharaoh would continue to resist, but God would show His power, both to Israel and to Egypt. The proof of His power would be in the signs and wonders displayed through the ten plagues.

Often when I've heard the stories of the plagues, I always assumed them to be punishment for Pharaoh's stubbornness. But we learn something interesting when God declares a fourth plague: Israel will be exempt from this one (Exodus 8:22). This means that Israel experienced the first three plagues right along the Egyptians. Their water turned to blood too. Their houses also filled with frogs and gnats.

Why do you think Israel was included in the first three plagues?

This revelation ushers in a new line of thought. If Israel also experienced the first few signs and wonders God did in Egypt, and they are the people God is seeking to set free, I'm not sure the plagues are meant to be a punishment. I think this is God revealing His power.

Remember, this generation of Israel spent their whole lives enslaved in Egypt, immersed in that culture. Egypt is a polytheistic society, which means they worshiped multiple gods. While Israel may not have participated in Egyptian worship, they were definitely surrounded by it. They were also under Pharaoh's thumb. It had been generations since they had experienced God's power. The plagues are God's way of offering judgement on Egypt, while also reminding Israel who He is.

What do these first three plagues reveal to you about who God is?

God is stronger than any Egyptian god. He is more powerful than Pharaoh. He is not a senseless, stone-faced deity, like those worshiped in Egyptian temples. God knows and loves His people. He makes a distinction among them and when the fourth plague begins, Israel is not affected by it.

As we move through these next few chapters, it may be difficult to see God's goodness and love, but the same loving God we see in the New Testament, we also see

WEEK TWO

in the Old Testament. God's love is here in Exodus, we just may need to rethink our ideas about love. To do that, we're going to jump to the New Testament for a moment.

Read 1 Corinthians 13. What does this chapter teach us about what love looks like?

How do you see God's love playing out in what we've read of Exodus so far?

On the surface, God's love may not seem apparent, but it is here.

God, in His love, is fighting for His people. He isn't ripping them out of the only home they've lived in, but He is building trust with them, showing them His power. Even when the people doubt, God keeps His promise to free them.

We also see God's love in how He handles the Egyptians and Pharaoh. He could have struck Pharaoh down right on the spot the first time he refused to let Israel go, but in His love, God sends plagues, providing Pharaoh and the other Egyptians the opportunity to surrender and trust Him. The Lord wants both Israel and Egypt to know that He is God, the one true God.

Every step of the way, God is consistent in His nature. As we explored a few lessons ago, God is not swayed by doubt. Rather, He enters into the doubt and reminds us of His faithfulness. God is not threatened by powerful men or ruling powers. He is more powerful, and He is willing to fight for His people.

As much as I wish Israel's journey into freedom was clean-cut and simple, there is more going on here. The account of the plagues will be one of those stories that spread to neighboring people groups. Israel, Egypt, and other nations will talk about this experience as one where God revealed His power and authority. Up to this point in Scripture, God has been revealing Himself to individuals. Now, God is making

Himself known to entire nations. He will lead Israel out of Egypt with His strong right hand, and Egypt will not soon forget it.

How does seeing God's power in today's reading encourage you in your own freedom journey?

How have you experienced God's power in the past? How has that experience impacted your faith?

In what ways do you need to know God's power in your own life right now?

Day 9: The Lord is Great

MEDITATE ON PSALM 135:5-14

The Exodus is a defining moment in Israel's history, and as such, it is a story that is recounted and retold throughout the rest of Scripture. God's victory in leading Israel out of Egypt is a commonly referenced in the Psalms. Often the Exodus is an event used to call the people to praise. In today's Scripture meditation, we're reading a portion of a Psalm that celebrates the work God did, His power, and His sovereignty.

Prepare: Be still before the Lord. Ask Him to prepare your heart to read and engage with this Scripture. Lay your heart open before Him and ask Him to speak.

Read the Word: Read the passage slowly. What words or phrases stand out to you?

Meditate on the Word: Read the passage again. How does this word or phrase connect to your life?

Respond to the Word: Read the passage again. Be honest with God about your response to this word and passage. How do you feel about it? What are you thinking? How are you responding to God? How is God inviting you to respond?

Rest in the Word: Read the passage one more time. Simply rest in God's Word. Submit yourself to His presence and just be present with Him.

Live the Word: How will you live into what you read and heard today?

Day 10: Hardened Hearts

STUDY EXODUS 9-10

....

....

I think now is a good time to tackle the elephant in the room—the question that is often quick to rise up when we read this narrative of Pharaoh's reaction to the plagues. Well, maybe it hasn't crossed your mind yet, but it's definitely crossed mine.

Why is the Lord judging Pharaoh if the Lord is the one hardening Pharaoh's heart?

I've asked that question before in my own reading of these passages. After each plague, when Pharaoh calls Moses and asks him to pray to God and put an end to the plague, there is a statement made about Pharaoh's hard heart. We're told in Scripture that God is good and that He is love, so why does it seem like He is manipulating Pharaoh in order to free Israel? Does God only love Israel and not Egypt?

It can be easy to fall into this line of thinking because of the phrasing that's used when Scripture says that the Lord hardened Pharaoh's heart. We read it as an act God is doing, instead of the result of Pharaoh's interactions with the Lord. Yes, God is responsible for the events at hand, but Pharaoh is accountable for his actions and responses.[3]

In order to address this concern, let's jump backwards a bit and track Pharaoh's responses to God and His people. We're going to go all the way back to Exodus 1. As we work our way forward, let's take note of Pharaoh's responses and the language that is used to describe the state of his heart.

Our first encounter with Pharaoh is in Exodus 1:8-10. Look back at this passage. What is Pharaoh's response to Israel?

Threatened by Israel's power, Pharaoh enacts a plan to subdue the people. He hardens his own heart here, and God responds. Exodus 2-3 details God's response to Pharaoh's oppression over Israel by calling Moses to lead Israel out of Egypt.

In Exodus 5, we meet Pharaoh again. Moses and Aaron approach the Egyptian king with a message from the Lord. What is Pharaoh's response to Moses' request that he let Israel go?

Again, Pharaoh hardens his heart. He claims to have no knowledge of this God Moses is talking about, and again, Pharaoh seems to feel threatened. Rather than freeing the people, Pharaoh heaps more work on them. And that is when the plagues begin. The Lord tells Moses in Exodus 7:14 that Pharaoh's heart is hard, and as a sign of His power, God turns the water to blood.

WEEK TWO

What is Pharaoh's response (verses 22-23)?

Next, God sends frogs. This time Pharaoh asks for relief, but once that relief comes, what is his response (Exodus 8:15)?

What is his response to the gnats (8:19)?

What is his response to the flies (8:32)?

Over and over and over again, Pharaoh has the opportunity to turn and repent, to let Israel go free. As the plagues become more severe, and more of the nation is destroyed, it almost looks like Pharaoh may finally relent. He even goes so far as to confess his sin (Exodus 9:27, 10:17), but once he feels relief from the plagues, Pharaoh changes his mind. He is playing the system. God knows it. Moses knows it. Pharaoh is still determined to keep a tight hold on Israel.

While God is passing judgment on the nation of Egypt for their treatment of His people, Pharaoh is accountable for his unwillingness to relent. During these first five plagues, he refuses to humble himself before the Lord and, as we'll see in the next few chapters, that will result in a tremendous amount of loss—both personally and nationally.

After all of this, we see a change in language. Now, during the second five plagues, it is God who is hardening Pharaoh's heart. Pharaoh has reached the point of no return. He is so evil, so unwilling to humble Himself before God, that God uses the state of Pharaoh's heart to accomplish His will.[4]

So what does all of this have to do with us and our own journey to living in the freedom God invites us to live in?

Well, first of all, I think this paints God in a very gracious light. While that statement of hardening Pharaoh's heart may have shaken our confidence in His character, we've seen that God, in His grace, gave Pharaoh multiple opportunities to repent and do the right thing. Even though God knew how things would play out, He gives Pharaoh the dignity of making his own choices. We also see God's justice in continuing to judge Israel, and specifically Pharaoh, for his treatment of Israel. These first ten chapters establish the character of God, which is something we will continue to explore throughout the remainder of this study.

Knowing God's character is essential. If Israel is going to follow God into freedom, they need to be reminded of the kind of God He is. The same is true for us. This journey into freedom is messy, hard, and long. If we're going to enter into it, if we're going to ask God to free us from the things holding us captive, we need to trust the One who rescues us and leads us into freedom. We need to trust that He is faithful and that, even when we don't understand His methods, He is good.

Tracking Pharaoh's heart responses also urges use to check-in with our own hearts. Are we resisting God in any way? Are we fighting against the freedom He wants to give? Is there any hardness in our hearts that we need to repent of?

We'll close our time of study today by taking time to reflect on these things.

Are there any ways you are hardening your heart toward God?

WEEK TWO

Take time to confess any resentment, distrust, or doubt you've been carrying about God's character or ways.

Ask God to soften your heart and increase your faith in His goodness and grace.

Day 11: Search My Heart

MEDITATE ON PSALM 139:23-24

Taking time to examine our hearts and confess any hardness we find there is a beneficial practice. However, there are times when we don't even know that our hearts have become hard. That's why inviting God and giving Him permission to bring things to the surface is an important part of the practice of self-examination. For today's Scripture meditation we are back in Psalm 139. We're going to lean into the closing verses of this Psalm and pray right along with David, "Search my heart, Lord."

Prepare: Be still before the Lord. Ask Him to prepare your heart to read and engage with this Scripture. Lay your heart open before Him and ask Him to speak.

Read the Word: Read the passage slowly. What words or phrases stand out to you?

Meditate on the Word: Read the passage again. How does this word or phrase connect to your life?

Respond to the Word: Read the passage again. Be honest with God about your response to this word and passage. How do you feel about it? What are you thinking? How are you responding to God? How is God inviting you to respond?

Rest in the Word: Read the passage one more time. Simply rest in God's Word. Submit yourself to His presence and just be present with Him.

Live the Word: How will you live into what you read and heard today?

Day 12: A Rhythm of Remembrance

STUDY EXODUS 11-12

We're nearing the climax of Israel's Exodus story. Plagues sent by God have ravaged the land of Egypt. Israel and Egypt have seen God's powerful hand stretched out against Pharaoh, who is still sitting in stubborn refusal. Everything has been building to this final plague, to Passover. Pharaoh is told exactly what is about to happen and he is given one more opportunity to let Israel go, but he still refuses.

What will this final plague be?

FINALLY FREE

When Moses leaves Pharaoh, he returns to the Israelites and helps them prepare for what is coming. Freedom is nearly in their grasp, they just have to trust the Lord to deliver on His promise.

The evening of Passover, families gather together in their homes, their door frames painted with the blood of the lamb they killed for their supper feast. They eat with their sandals on, their cloaks wrapped around them, and their staff in hand. They are ready to move when they are given the word.

At midnight, just as the Lord said, He moves through the land, taking the lives of all the Egyptian firstborns, but passing over the Hebrew homes covered in lamb's blood. In one night, God enacts His final judgement on Egypt's gods, and the death of Pharaoh's son is the final straw. Pharaoh finally relents and releases Israel. The Egyptians, who had witnessed the power of God, send the people out with all their wealth, and four hundred and thirty years to the day, the people of Israel leave Egypt and take their first steps into freedom.

How do you think that must have felt for Israel to see God finally come through on His promise?

With their new freedom, God gives Israel a command: Passover is to be a yearly ceremony for the people. Each year they are to share the meal together and tell the story of how God came through for them. Passover will be a regular rhythm in their community, a rhythm of remembering and celebrating when God set them free.

A few years ago, my small group celebrated Passover together. We sat around a long table with all of the elements of the meal spread out before us, and we were led through the unhurried ceremony. The fascinating thing about celebrating Passover as a Christian is seeing how this ceremony ties to Jesus.

Nothing God does it by accident. Everything has intention and multiple levels of meaning.

God chose Israel to be His people, the nation descended from Abraham and the family through whom He chose to bring blessing to the whole world. God freed them from captivity and gave them a rhythm of remembrance so that every year, when the anniversary of the Exodus came, they could remember again what God had done. Each generation would hear about the wonders of the Lord and His mighty hand that set them free from Pharaoh's tyranny.

But Passover was just a shadow of what was to come.

Generations later, a descendent of Abraham would be born—Jesus. His life would also be threatened by the command of a power-hungry and paranoid king who ordered the death of Hebrew babies. Jesus would grow up and speak the words of the Lord to the people, telling them of God's goodness and His promise of freedom. Like Moses, Jesus would offer instructions for a ceremony of remembrance, taking the familiar Passover meal and forming it into something more—something complete.

Read Luke 22:7-23. What similarities do you notice between Passover and the first Communion?

Like Passover, Communion was given as a sign of remembrance. Like Passover, the disciples are given instructions to "do this in remembrance" before they even realized what they were being instructed to remember.

The day after that first Communion, Jesus was led to the top of a hill just outside of Jerusalem, where He was nailed to the cross. He became like that Passover lamb, whose blood covered us and protected us from God's judgment of sin. Like Israel's Exodus out of that foreign land of Egypt, when Jesus rose from the dead and walked out of the tomb three days later, He walked us into the freedom of eternal life without condemnation.

When we think of freedom, we view it as a release from the things that have held us captive. That's what Israel was waiting for, and that is part of the freedom journey. But whenever we're freed *from* something, that release allows us to walk *in* the freedom of something new.

We are set free to live free (Galatians 5:1).

And when we are set free, we are instructed to remember.

When we're no longer desperate to be set free, we humans are liable to forget. We're prone to wander off and live our own way, but God wants us to remember that He is the source of our freedom and the goal of our freedom. We are set free to live freely in relationship with Him. The freedom our souls long for is only found in Him.

In the coming chapters, we'll see how Israel's freedom from Egypt makes space for them to step into the new life and new abundance God has for them. But for now, let's bask in the wonder of what has happened here. God did it! He really did it! After generations in Egypt, Israel is walking out as a free nation.

What is most impactful for you about Israel's freedom from Egypt?

Do you have any rhythms in your life to help you remember what God has done? Consider any anniversaries, habits, end of the year rhythms, or spiritual disciplines you incorporate in your life. How might you add rhythms of remembrance into your life?

Day 13: Past Faithfulness, Present Faith

MEDITATE ON PSALM 77:11-15

Remembering God's past faithfulness feeds our present faith. When we are able to look back and remember how God came through, how He acted, what He revealed to us, those things become faith markers for us—places where we are sure beyond a shadow of a doubt about who God is and what He does. Remembering reminds us that the God we serve is consistent. Even as we walk into the unknown, we can trust that the God who moved before will move again.

Prepare: Be still before the Lord. Ask Him to prepare your heart to read and engage with this Scripture. Lay your heart open before Him and ask Him to speak.

Read the Word: Read the passage slowly. What words or phrases stand out to you?

Meditate on the Word: Read the passage again. How does this word or phrase connect to your life?

Respond to the Word: Read the passage again. Be honest with God about your response to this word and passage. How do you feel about it? What are you thinking? How are you responding to God? How is God inviting you to respond?

Rest in the Word: Read the passage one more time. Simply rest in God's Word. Submit yourself to His presence and just be present with Him.

Live the Word: How will you live into what you read and heard today?

Day 14: Prepare for Rest

SABBATH

There have been seasons in my life when Sabbath is especially difficult—when my to-do list is a mile long or my bank account is low and another day of work seems like it would help out a lot. It can be tempting to let my day of rest become another day of productivity and accomplishment, but I notice the difference when I give into the work instead of giving into the rest. I end up a lot more tired, anxious, stressed, and feeling distant from God.

God calls us to rest and He established a rhythm in which we can do that. In fact, He models rest for us. After doing the work of creating the world and everything in it, He took a day of rest (Genesis 2:1-3). The fascinating thing is that that day of rest was also the first full day that Adam and Eve experienced after God breathed life into them. On day six, God makes humans and on day seven, He establishes a day of rest for Himself and His creation.

Sabbath is a holistic rhythm that makes space for our minds, hearts, bodies, and souls to rest on a regular basis. When we practice Sabbath, we enter into the rhythms of life in which God created this world to function, but sometimes resting well requires a little bit of planning.

The longer I practice Sabbath, the more Sabbath becomes the climax of my week. Sabbath is not the reward for a week of hard work. All of the work I do is done as I look toward Sabbath. I've started planning my week around my day of rest. Sabbath is the first thing I write in on my calendar each week. I've also learned what I need in order to rest well, so I make sure to schedule in time to prepare for my Sabbath. I like a checked off to-do list and a clean space. I also like to make sure my heart and body are prepared for rest.

Since I practice Sabbath on Saturday, Thursday is usually when I begin preparing. I look over my list for the week and make decisions about what needs to be finished before the end of the week. I also make decisions about what tasks will need to move to the next week or need to wait until after Sabbath. I assess my house and make note of any chores, cleaning, or tidying-up that I want to do to prepare my space for rest. Laundry and dishes are almost always on the list. I also make plans for Sabbath meals. I love cooking and eating good food on my day of rest, so that often means a trip to the grocery store.

It's also important for me to prepare my mind and body for Sabbath. The night before Sabbath, I give myself some letdown time—a period in the evening when the work is done and I'm getting into the rhythm of rest. I take a hot shower, get into some comfy pajamas, then sit down with my journal to take stock of my heart and my internal world. I reflect on my week, where I saw God moving and working, I make space for confession and I surrender the things weighing on my heart and mind.

Sabbath preparation isn't about fixing or finishing everything. It's about making space and surrendering myself and my time to God. There are many weeks where I walk into Sabbath with unfinished to-do lists and very little time to prepare myself for Sabbath, but even then, I make the effort to stop and rest. We'll talk more next week about what it looks like to surrender to Sabbath, but for now, let's make some plans to prepare for Sabbath this week.

You already did the hard part last week by deciding what day you will practice Sabbath and what Sabbath will and will not include. We're going to keep that rhythm this week and build on it.

WEEK TWO

In addition to keeping your Sabbath boundaries, let's make some plans to help you prepare for your day of rest. Consider the questions below and then add your Sabbath preparations to your plans for the week.

What do I find restful? What makes me feel most like myself? What makes me come alive and fills me up?

How will I prepare my house and space for Sabbath?

How will I prepare my heart and body for Sabbath?

When will I make space in my schedule to prepare for Sabbath?

How will I mark the end of the work week and begin to transition into Sabbath?

Even with planning and preparing, there will be some weeks when life happens and your Sabbath preparations aren't completed. Remember, the goal of Sabbath is to connect with God, not perfect this practice. When our plans fail or our preparation feels incomplete, we need to give ourselves grace and make the choice to rest anyway.

Choose a grace statement from one of mine below or create your own to repeat to yourself when Sabbath comes before the work is done.

The work will still be there after the Sabbath.

I am a human being, not a human doing. Enjoy being for a while.

God takes care of me. I can trust Him even when the work isn't finished.

My ability to complete work does not define me. Jesus does, and He says I am dearly loved.

SABBATH REFLECTION

How did Sabbath go for you this week?

Did you notice any differences in how Sabbath felt this week compared to last week?

How did Sabbath prep go for you?

WEEK TWO

Was there anything that didn't get done before Sabbath that you wish had been? How did you handle that?

How will you continue to shape your Sabbath preparation for next time?

Week Three

Day 15: Trusting the Way-Maker

STUDY EXODUS 13-14

One of the things I want you to pay attention to as we move forward from this point is how God interacts with His people. Israel has just been freed from slavery, and that's exciting, but the greatest battle is ahead. All these people have ever known is slavery and scarcity. Their lives have been defined by endless work. Now they must learn what it looks like to step into the abundance and rest God offers. They must learn what it means to live as God's people, as His children.

As we talked about in our last lesson, part of living as God's children is remembering the work He has done in our lives.

How does God build rhythms of remembrance into their lives for this new nation of Israel?

It is so interesting to me that the first commands and instructions God gives Israel have to do with celebrations. God is establishing Himself as a different kind of ruler than Pharaoh. He is not the God who demands labor. He is the God of rest.

On the tail of the instructions about the Passover celebration, Israel is given instructions about another feast—the Feast of Unleavened Bread. This festival was to be celebrated the seven days after Passover. Israel is to remember their deliverance from Egypt, not just for one day, but an entire week. As you continue through these first few books of the Old Testament, you will encounter several other celebrations and rhythms that God weaves into the Jewish calendar. Their lives are to be marked by regular periods of rest and celebration.

God is also establishing this idea that Israel is to be a nation set-apart. That's what the consecration of the firstborn is all about. While the tenth plague claimed the lives of the Egyptian firstborns, God is making a way for Israel's firstborns to be redeemed.

After establishing these new rhythms and expectations, the author gives us a peek behind the current at the journey Israel is embarking on.

Look again at Exodus 13:17-22. What interesting thing do you notice about the direction God leads Israel once they get out of Egypt? What is His reasoning for taking this particular path?

I remember the first time I understood what was happening in this passage when God leads the people through this less direct route. My heart softened a little more toward the God who didn't want Israel giving up right out of the gate. While the direct route to the land of Canaan would save them time, God knew the Philistines would intimidate the people and send them running back to Egypt. True, the longer way took them more time and led them to the Red Sea, but God chose this route intentionally with Israel's good in mind.

Sometimes we need to allow God to lead us the long way.

WEEK THREE

Israel doesn't seem to mind until they are bookended by the Red Sea and Pharaoh's approaching army. After the shock of grief had run its course, Pharaoh realizes he has made a mistake in allowing his labor force to go free, so he gathers up his chariots and his army and goes after them. And Israel freaks out!

What is Israel's response to Pharaoh's approaching army?

It seemed to Israel that they had gone from a bad situation to a much worse one. Was it not enough for them to die in Egypt? Did God have to bring them into the wilderness to kill them off? Whatever trust they have built with God thus far is put into question. They see no way out. But like the popular worship song says, God is a way-maker. Even where there seems to be no way, God makes a way.

What does Moses tell Israel in response to their fear?

How does God make a way for Israel to escape?

In a powerful display, the pillar of cloud and fire that has led Israel this far, moves behind the people and becomes a fiery barrier between them and Pharaoh's army. All night a wind blows, driving the waters of the Red Sea aside and creating a dry path for Israel to walk across on. With walls of water on either side of them, the entire nation of Israel crosses the sea without leaving a single muddy footprint, and once they make it to the other side, the waters crash in and swallow up Pharaoh and his chariots.

FINALLY FREE

The fear Israel had about having to return to Egypt—the fear that their freedom was too good to be true—are swallowed up in the sea, just like their enemies. God came through for them again. He saved His people. Now the work begins to remake them from the slaves they thought they were into the children of God He created them to be.

In what ways have you doubted God's ability to take care of you?

What is your response when you're facing trouble? Is it to get loud and panic? Or to get quiet and trust?

What encouragement do you find for your own freedom journey in Israel's experience at the Red Sea?

Day 16: A Way in the Wilderness

MEDITATE ON ISAIAH 43:18-19

There may be times on our freedom journey when we fear we have reached the end of our rope. We're stuck with nowhere else to go. When that happens, we need to lean into the One who makes a way even when there seems to be no way. In today's Scripture meditation, we're going to focus on a passage that reminds us of what God did at the Red Sea and that there are still greater things God will do.

Prepare: Be still before the Lord. Ask Him to prepare your heart to read and engage with this Scripture. Lay your heart open before Him and ask Him to speak.

Read the Word: Read the passage slowly. What words or phrases stand out to you?

Meditate on the Word: Read the passage again. How does this word or phrase connect to your life?

Respond to the Word: Read the passage again. Be honest with God about your response to this word and passage. How do you feel about it? What are you thinking? How are you responding to God? How is God inviting you to respond?

Rest in the Word: Read the passage one more time. Simply rest in God's Word. Submit yourself to His presence. Just be present with Him.

Live the Word: How will you live into what you read and heard today?

Day 17: The Fullness of Freedom

STUDY EXODUS 15-16

....

....

Israel has just witnessed something miraculous! The Egyptians and their horses were swallowed up in the Red Sea, though Israel crossed on dry ground. They may have doubted God's motivation in freeing them from Egypt when they came to the water and saw Pharaoh's army on their tail, but they cried out for help, then they waited and watched as God came through.

Now they are free! Really free! Truly free! And that is something worth celebrating!

How does Israel celebrate their newfound freedom?

FINALLY FREE

If you've seen the DreamWorks Production of *The Prince of Egypt*, the final scene of the movie shows Israel on the other side of the Red Sea as the water crashes in on Pharaoh's army. First, the people are silent and shocked, then reality settles in. They sing, they celebrate, and the credits roll. We like to think of this as the end of the Exodus story, and I guess in some ways it is, but it is not the end of Israel's freedom story.

Remember, the main purpose of being freed *from* is to be free *for* something new and better.

While Israel's freedom from Egypt is a huge deal, this is simply the beginning of the story. There are a lot more chapters left in the book of Exodus. For the rest of the book, we're going to focus on what it looks like for Israel to embrace their new freedom as well as the challenges they face as they begin to live into their identity as God's nation.

From the Red Sea, God begins to lead Israel through the wilderness, and things become difficult. They don't find any water for three days, and when they finally do, the water is bitter and undrinkable. Moses, being the figurehead and leader, receives the brunt of their complaints as the people cry out, "What will we drink?" (Exodus 15:24). Moses takes their need before the Lord and He answers in a surprising way.

How is the water problem solved?

When I studied this passage with my small group, it just about broke me. On first read, at least for me, this just seems like a quirky little story about how Israel doesn't trust God to provide for them. They may have witnessed His wonders in Egypt, and they saw Him save them from Pharaoh's army just three days before, but they are only beginning to get to know God's character. Knowing Him as the God who rescues, doesn't mean they know Him as a God who will meet their needs.

They needed water, and the Lord provided a way to make the water drinkable.

But that's not all. When my small group studied this section of Exodus, one of the people in our group noted something that changed how I read this account at Marah

WEEK THREE

as well as the rest of Exodus.

Take another look at Exodus 16 verse 26:

He said, "If you will carefully obey the LORD your God, do what is right in his sight, pay attention to his commands, and keep all his statutes, I will not inflict any illnesses on you that I inflicted on the Egyptians. For I am the LORD who heals you."

After God makes the water clean and encourages the people to follow Him, He reveals another aspect of His character: *"For I am the Lord who heals you."*

The experience at Marah wasn't just about the water. Yes, the people were thirsty and God provided something to drink, but He also brought them to a literal place of healing. He brought them to this place they called "bitter" to heal the bitterness in their hearts. He provides an object lesson, showing them that, just as He made the water clean, He will make their hearts clean. It will take time. Bitterness can be hard to uproot. It will also require intentionality on their part. They have to commit to Him. They have to obey Him. They also have to trust His character.

God did not bring them into the wilderness to die, though this will be a line of thought they continue to give in to. No, He brought them out of Egypt to bring them into the abundant life He created them for. They were not made to be slaves. They were made to be whole people who lived holy lives. But before they could recognize who they were and live into that identity as God's people, they needed a crash course in God's heart and His character.

Bitterness had to be rooted out. These people who had faced a lifetime of trauma needed healing. God led them out of Egypt and into the wilderness to begin healing the deep brokenness that permeated the entire nation.

The experience at Marah is just the first of many experiences where their faith and beliefs about God are put to the test.

Not too long after the water incident, the people become hungry. The provisions they had when they came out of Egypt are just about used up. With fear, anger, and grumbling stomachs, they approach Moses again, complaining that their basic needs aren't being met. They might have been slaves in Egypt, but at least they had food. They still see God as a Pharaoh figure, one who will use them and cast them aside at His will. Again, God proves them wrong and meets their needs.

How does the Lord provide for Israel this time?

God's provision also comes with a practice of trust. Manna will be available with the dew each morning. The people are to go out and gather manna for six days. No one is to stockpile it; it will only last the day and then become rancid. On the sixth day they are to gather enough of the manna for two days, because on the seventh day it is Sabbath and there will be no manna on the ground.

There are a lot of layers of trust being built here. Israel must trust that the manna will show up each morning. They are completely dependent on God's provision, and if they try to save any manna for the next day, it will spoil. They also have to trust that the second days' worth of manna they gather before Sabbath will not spoil and they will have enough to eat on the Sabbath.

God is completely rewiring how Israel believes life works. Their performance does not determine whether or not they are provided for. Their work does not prove their worth. They are God's people, worthy of rest and recipients of God's protection and provision.

Exodus is a book of freedom *and* of healing. You can't have one without the other. God knew—He knows—that even if a body is physically free from bondage, the heart and mind of a person can still be enslaved. Israel's physical freedom is only the beginning of the freeing work God wants to do in His people.

Are you carrying any bitterness in your heart that needs God's healing? Confess that and ask Him to make your heart free.

WEEK THREE

What do you believe about God's care for you? Do you believe that He will provide enough for you? Are there any areas in which you doubt God's provision in your life or feel pressure to take care of yourself?

Day 18: Look at the Birds

MEDITATE ON MATTHEW 6:25-33

....

When it comes to trusting God's provision and care for us, there are few passages I revisit more often than the verses at the end of Matthew 6. This passage is tucked into the middle of Jesus' Sermon on the Mount. For three chapters, Jesus teaches the people what the kingdom of God looks like, and what it looks like to live holy lives. A big piece of that is trusting God to take care of us. In today's Scripture meditation, we're going to lean in and listen to the words of Jesus and learn what it means to trust God to meet our needs.

Prepare: Be still before the Lord. Ask Him to prepare your heart to read and engage with this Scripture. Lay your heart open before Him and ask Him to speak.

Read the Word: Read the passage slowly. What words or phrases stand out to you?

Meditate on the Word: Read the passage again. How does this word or phrase connect to your life?

Respond to the Word: Read the passage again. Be honest with God about your response to this word and passage. How do you feel about it? What are you thinking? How are you responding to God? How is God inviting you to respond?

Rest in the Word: Read the passage one more time. Simply rest in God's Word. Submit yourself to His presence and just be present with Him.

Live the Word: How will you live into what you read and heard today?

Day 19: Do Not Test the Lord

STUDY EXODUS 17-18

Do you kind of feel like history is repeating itself with today's passage? The situation of Israel running out of water and complaining about it may feel similar. However, as I read, I get the feeling that things are different here. Let's look at these two passages with Israel's complaints and see if we can notice any differences.

Read Exodus 15:22-27. How do Israel, Moses, and God interact in this water story?

Israel

Moses

God

Now reread Exodus 17:1-7. How do Israel, Moses, and God interact in this water story? How do they interact differently than in the first experience?

Israel

Moses

God

WEEK THREE

In Exodus 15, Israel was still new to trusting God to provide for their needs. We talked in our last lesson about how they were learning to trust God, not only as rescuer, but also as their healer and provider. In Exodus 17, however, they have been traveling with God for a bit. They've been following His cloud by day and fire by night. They drank the water at Marah that God made drinkable and they ate the quail and manna the Lord provided for them. Israel has seen God's provision. They have experienced His care for them, yet they still doubt Him. Or perhaps they just refuse to trust Him wholeheartedly, which is why Moses gets angry when they cry to him for water again.

Did you notice the addition this time to Israel's argument? In Exodus 15:24, Israel simply asked what they would drink. In Exodus 17, however, Israel demands water (verse 2) and accuses Moses and the Lord for bringing them out of Egypt to die in the wilderness (verse 3). They also call into question the promise of God's presence since their needs aren't immediately being met (verse 7).

Even with the long list of miraculous ways God has shown up for them, the hearts of the people of Israel have become hard. Maybe their freedom has made them feel a bit entitled. Maybe God just isn't working fast enough for them. Maybe they are weary and crabby from traveling too long. Whatever the reason, this is one of the defining moments in Israel's history. The Lord still shows up for infant Israel. He still provides water for them, but this experience at Meribah and Massah becomes the example of what not to do. In fact, this experience will be referred to often in Israel's narrative because of how they test God here. The writer of Psalm 95:8-9 clearly commands his readers not to follow Israel's example:

> *Do not harden your hearts as at Meribah,*
> *as on that day at Massah in the wilderness*
> *where your ancestors tested me;*
> *they tried me, though they had seen what I did.*

Now, I do want to insert a quick note here, because I don't want us to confuse testing God with seeking confirmation from Him. There is a difference. Israel is reprimanded here because, in their hearts, they did not believe God will take care of them. They challenge His character and forgot everything He has already shown them. This differs from their first experience where they needed proof of God's care.

I think it's okay to ask for proof. I think it's okay for us to ask God to show us His goodness in physical and tangible ways. However, there comes a point when we have to act on faith. There comes a point when we need to check our hearts and assess why we are asking for or demanding things from God. Do we feel entitled? Have our hearts hardened toward Him? Are we seeking self-sufficiency and stuff or are we seeking and desiring God?

The journey into freedom leaves us vulnerable to pride and entitlement. It leaves us open to doubt. We may be tempted to test the Lord, to question His character and His care, but let's not be like Israel in this way. Let's not let our hearts grow hard toward the Lord.

It's going to be hard sometimes to trust God to do what He's said He would do, to take care of us and to keep being faithful, but that's kind of the point of faith—trusting even before we see the outcome. Trusting even when we feel like we're in a tight and desperate place. That is the only way we will truly experience the rest and abundance God has for us, because both rest and abundance are found in His presence and in relationship with Him.

Read Psalm 95. What warnings does the Psalmist provide in relation to Israel's experience at Meribah? How might you take those warnings to heart, not out of fear, but from a place of trust in who God is?

Take a heart check. Are you approaching God to test Him or are seeking to know Him better?

Day 20: Test Your Faith

MEDITATE ON JAMES 1:2-6

While we are discouraged from putting God to the test, as Israel did, it is important to test our faith. Where are we staking our trust? What are we expecting of God? Are we actually leaning into Him, or just keeping Him around for the occasional miracle? Allowing our faith to be tested will strengthen our relationship with God. In today's Scripture meditation, we're going to settle into this faith space.

Prepare: Be still before the Lord. Ask Him to prepare your heart to read and engage with this Scripture. Lay your heart open before Him and ask Him to speak.

Read the Word: Read the passage slowly. What words or phrases stand out to you?

Meditate on the Word: Read the passage again. How does this word or phrase connect to your life?

Respond to the Word: Read the passage again. Be honest with God about your response to this word and passage. How do you feel about it? What are you thinking? How are you responding to God? How is God inviting you to respond?

Rest in the Word: Read the passage one more time. Simply rest in God's Word. Submit yourself to His presence and just be present with Him.

Live the Word: How will you live into what you read and heard today?

Day 21: Surrender to Rest

SABBATH

Sabbath is both an invitation and an obligation. For Israel, a weekly Sabbath and regular practices of rest and celebration were woven into their laws. It was what set them apart from other nations.

God knows that rest and ceasing from striving is what is best for us. He won't force it on us, but He does invite us into it. However, Sabbath isn't just about getting the rest we need. This weekly rhythm is an acknowledgement of who God is. It is a celebration of His character and a declaration of our trust in Him. Sabbath is God's day and it is a holy space to remember who we are and who God is.

Embracing Sabbath is an unusual thing in our culture, even within some Christian circles. We think that to get ahead and to be successful we need to keep the momentum going. We rest only to get the energy we need to keep working, or we treat rest as a reward for a job well-done and something we can't indulge in until the work is done. Sabbath was designed to be an untwisting of our identities from our work and a reminder that it is not by our own hands that we are cared for, but by the grace of God. He gives us everything we need, including rest.

Part of the rhythm of Sabbath requires us to surrender to that rest. It requires us to surrender our time, our lists, the expectations we have of ourselves, our needs, our finances, our work, and the things we tend to find our value in and press into a day that is all about God. Sabbath is a reminder that our time is not our own; it is God's. It is a reminder to do as Jesus says in Matthew 11:28-30 and let our weary and heavy-laden souls come and find rest in Him.

In the last two weeks you've prayerfully made some decisions and plans around your Sabbath to help you rest well. This week I'm going to invite you to enter into the movement of Sabbath where we surrender to this time of rest.

Surrendering can be both a physical act and a habit of the heart. We surrender our time, our bodies, our space, and our whole selves to God.

This movement of surrender is what marks the beginning of Sabbath. It is where we lay down the work of the week and we take up the rest God offers us. This surrendering piece can be messy and hard, but it is good. I find it helpful to pair the act of surrendering with a physical act. There are a few ways I like to do this. I'll write down all my concerns in my journal, allowing the act of naming all those things to be my act of surrender. Sometimes I will close my eyes, open my hands, and breathe deeply in a posture of surrender. Sometimes I will pray, and with audible words surrender myself and my time to God.

The idea here is that you are transitioning into rest and leaving the work behind. This is the place where we make a hard stop on our work and we just rest. This is where we acknowledge that Sabbath is a time set apart for God and we surrender our time and our burdens back to Him.

As you prepare for Sabbath this week, take some time to think and pray about this aspect of surrender. How can you surrender to rest and Sabbath this week? In what way will you make Sabbath a set-apart space?

WEEK THREE

SABBATH REFLECTION

How did you incorporate the rhythm of surrender into Sabbath this week?

Did you make any changes from how you practiced Sabbath in the previous weeks?

Have you seen any changes in yourself since you began practicing Sabbath?

How has your relationship with God deepened over the last few weeks?

Week Four

Day 22: Consecrated for the Covenant

STUDY EXODUS 19-20

This is the point in Exodus where people generally start to tune out, but we're not going to do that. Paul writes in 2 Timothy 3:16, "All Scripture is inspired by God and is profitable for teaching, for rebuking, for correcting, for training in righteousness." That truth doesn't just apply to the parts of Scripture that we like or that are easy to understand. Paul says "*all* of Scripture." All means...well, all. Everything. Including the chapters of the Law, which we are stepping into today.

The first half of Exodus got us to the base of Mount Sinai. The last half of Exodus will focus on the instructions and laws God gives to the new nation of Israel. As we focus here for the remainder of our study, I want you to view this as a sort of scavenger hunt. We're on the search for truths about rest, abundance, and freedom. We're reading with the goal of knowing God better and seeing the heart of a Father who wants the best for His children.

Glance back through today's reading with this lens. In what ways do these three chapters teach us about freedom, rest, abundance, and God's Father-heart?

Three months have passed since Israel left Egypt. They've encountered God in different ways in the wilderness, and now we've come to the base of Mount Sinai.

We've been talking a lot about how the freedom God wants to give Israel—and us—is not just a physical freedom. The goal wasn't just to free the Israelites from slavery. If physical freedom was God's only aim, He would have been content to leave Israel on the other side Red Sea. Instead, we see Him continuing to lead the people, care for them, and provide for them. We see Him fulfilling His covenant to Abraham, and here at the base of Sinai, He enters into a new covenant with Israel, giving them the freedom to choose to be in relationship with Him.

This is an attribute of God I have grown to love. For much of my early Christian life, I believed there was one and only one way God wanted me to live, and I was bent on finding it. I was under the impression that I had to crack some sort of code in order to live in a way that was pleasing to Him. In recent years, however, God has revealed to me the beauty of choice. Yes, there are times when God is very clear about a decision to be made or a direction to go, but I am not His robot. I have the choice to obey or go my own way. I have the opportunity to choose Him and His plans or reject Him. Like Pharaoh and Israel, God gives us the dignity of choice. He makes Himself vulnerable to rejection so that, if we do choose relationship with Him, that relationship is between two parties who choose to be here, rather than a master lording over his slave.

Here at the base of Sinai, God makes the move to offer relationship to His people.

In Exodus 19:9-13, what does God tell Moses is about to happen? How are the people instructed to prepare for it?

WEEK FOUR

Consecrate isn't a word we use often in our modern language. Merriam-Webster defines the word *consecrate* this way: "to make or declare sacred; especially to devote irrevocably to the worship of God by a solemn practice."[6]

On the journey to Sinai, Israel has experienced God as their rescuer and provider. Now, they are about to experience Him as holy and worthy of worship and devotion. During this meeting at the mountain, when the people have bathed and consecrated themselves, God appears to them in the form of fire and cloud settling at the top of the mountain. He is continuing to reveal to them who He is. He is also setting Himself apart from the oppressive ruler they knew Pharaoh to be. Pharaoh was tyrannical and controlling, but God is holy, relational, and good.

That goodness looks a little different than we might expect. This image of God thundering from a cloud at the top of a mountain and setting clear boundaries that have deadly consequences if those boundaries are crossed doesn't exactly sound good. In fact, it sounds pretty scary. But God is entering into a covenant with Israel, and this is not something to take lightly. He is revealing Himself in a visible way and establishing these boundaries so that the people don't die. Death isn't what He wants for the people. He wants relationship, connection, and covenant.

God is about to deliver the Law to the people, and He wants them to be prepared. The last three months have been about giving Israel opportunities to trust Him, to trust His heart so that when they got here, they would be ready to receive the freedom of the Law. He wanted to make them ready to enter into this new covenant.

Once they are prepared, God speaks in the hearing of all the people and gives them the Ten Commandments. Every instruction and additional law that God will give to Moses and to Israel has its root in these ten things.

In your own words, outline the Ten Commandments below:

God begins these commands by establishing His identity: "I am the LORD your God, who brought you out of the land of Egypt, out of the place of slavery" (20:2). There are to be no other gods but Him. No one is to make idols or graven images of Him or any other gods, and no one may misuse His name. He is holy and He will be treated as such.

Walter Brueggemann makes an interesting point about these first three commandments in his book *Sabbath as Resistance*: "This claim of exclusiveness sounded at first like the exclusive claim of Pharaoh, for Pharaoh required absolute authority without any rival. But the exclusivity of YHWH [God] was different because of what followed. God spoke six times about the neighbor."[7]

While God does expect our full attention and commitment—and rightfully so—He spends much more time talking about Sabbath rest and what it looks like to love your neighbor.

These ten commands can really be summed up as three:

1. Love God

2. Rest well

3. Love people

When we're participating in these three things, we are living in freedom. We are able to experience the abundant life of knowing that we are loved and taken care of by God. He is in the rightful place in our lives and we are fully dependent upon Him. Because of that dependence, we can stop each week and rest, knowing we don't have to strive to take care of ourselves because God has already promised to do that. We can also rest from competing with those around us, trying to get ahead or prove ourselves more valuable than the next guy. We can rest from the constant pressure to see, do, or experience more because our value isn't found there. When we live from a place of loving God and resting well, that rest overflows into our ability to love others. We can value our neighbor, knowing that we are both equally loved and equally cared for by God. We don't have to compare our lives to theirs. We don't have to get what they have. We are safe. We are whole. We are loved. And we can share that truth with them.

Brueggemann sums this idea up well:

"You are in the image of the creator God who did not need to work to get ahead. Nor do you! God invites the ones at Sinai to a new life of neighborly freedom in which Sabbath is the cornerstone of faithful freedom."

These commands and the other laws to come aren't meant to box Israel in. They are meant to reestablish them as people who love and people who rest.

There are no gods like our God. He is the God who rescues and saves, the God who cares for and provides, the One who is holy and good. He cares about people, and He desires to be in committed relationship with His people.

And it is in that relationship where we find true freedom!

How do you view God? Does His holiness terrify you or comfort you? Do you fear and respect Him or are you afraid? Ask God to set you free and help you understand what His holiness means.

How has our study today shifted your view of the Ten Commandments?

Are there any areas of your life that you need to consecrate to the Lord?

Day 23: God's Covenant Love

MEDITATE ON JOHN 3:16-21

John 3 holds one of the most memorized and recited verses in all of Scripture. In today's Scripture meditation, we're going to focus on that verse and a handful of the verses that follow as we lean into the God who is defined by covenant love. In the Old Testament, God used individuals and the nation of Israel to introduce His covenant love to the world, but once Jesus steps on the scene, that covenant is extended to anyone and everyone who believes.

Prepare: Be still before the Lord. Ask Him to prepare your heart to read and engage with this Scripture. Lay your heart open before Him and ask Him to speak.

Read the Word: Read the passage slowly. What words or phrases stand out to you?

Meditate on the Word: Read the passage again. How does this word or phrase connect to your life?

Respond to the Word: Read the passage again. Be honest with God about your response to this word and passage. How do you feel about it? What are you thinking? How are you responding to God? How is God inviting you to respond?

Rest in the Word: Read the passage one more time. Simply rest in God's Word. Submit yourself to His presence and just be present with Him.

Live the Word: How will you live into what you read and heard today?

Day 24: Love God, Love People

STUDY EXODUS 21-23

In our previous lesson, we looked at how the Ten Commandments served as the framework of the Law for Israel. Now it's time to get into the nitty gritty of things. Today's reading is a bit lengthier, but I hope you stuck with it. I know Jewish laws regarding various areas of life aren't the most exciting to read, but one of the things I hope you find in the last half of this study is that, while we as Christians living in the New Covenant of Jesus are not required to live by these laws, they are still relevant. Remember what we said when we read the Ten Commandments? All of Scripture is helpful in knowing God, understanding His heart, and understanding how He created this world to function. That truth applies to these laws too.

The laws in today's passage focus mainly around two things: a more detailed looked at what it means to love your neighbor, and instructions for the Sabbath and feasts.

Let's start with loving your neighbor.

What has God already established about what it looks like for Israel to love their neighbor?

In Exodus 21, God begins this deeper discussion about loving neighbors. One aspect of this discussion is the treatment of slaves. Over and over again God has been reminding the people and establishing His identity as the God who brought them out of Egypt and out of slavery. He established Passover as a yearly reminder of God's saving grace and power. Israel's past identity as slaves, while it doesn't define them anymore, is supposed to affect how they treat people now. They know what it is like to be oppressed and burdened, and they are not to treat others that way.

Now, you might be wondering, why does God give laws about slaves at all? Why not just eliminate slavery from their way of life altogether? You're asking some great questions, and, honestly, I've asked them too.

When these kinds of questions arise and make us question God's character, we need to take some time to dig deeper instead of jumping to conclusions. Remember, the Bible was written in the context of a different culture and language, and sometimes things aren't as clear to us because we live in a different context.

The word that often gets translated as "slave" in our English Bibles is the Hebrew word *ebed*, which means bondservant.[8] In this context, the position as a bondservant was a temporary position for Israelites experiencing extreme hardship. The master-servant relationship God is laying out here isn't related to those who were kidnapped and forcefully taken and sold into slavery. The slavery or servitude we're talking about here, is actually a form of provision for the Israelite struggling to get their needs met. In those situations, an Israelite can enter into an agreement with a wealthier household to live as a bondservant for a set amount of time. The master's role is to treat that person fairly and provide for his or her needs. Then, once the amount of time has been fulfilled, the bondservant is to go free (Exodus 21:2). Understanding this context suddenly makes these laws very dignifying for those servants. They are not property; they are humans worthy of fair and generous treatment. Not only that, but this law further emphasizes the importance of community and loving their neighbors.

WEEK FOUR

God didn't free Israel so that they could live however they want. They are to pass on the kindness given to them through grace.

In what other ways does God instruct Israel to treat people with kindness, dignity, and grace?

The treatment of bondservants is not the only way God asks them to extend grace in their community. They are also to live differently when it comes to dealing with issues of restitution. If a person's property is taken or harmed in some way, the one in the wrong is to make it right. Depending on the property or item in question, God has provided laws to make sure that the one who has been wronged is taken care of.

We also see God's grace extended in the area of social justice. God's laws here provide protection and justice for the vulnerable, including women, foreigners, and the poor.

What do all of these laws about the treatment of people reveal to you about God's heart?

The Law isn't boring. It may be difficult to read at times, but when you allow the Law to instruct you about the heart of God, these chapters—and even the book of Leviticus—become rich with God's grace, love, and kindness.

This section of the Law finishes with more guidance for Sabbath practices and the observance of the festivals that will provide the rhythm for Israel's year. It should be no surprise at this point that Sabbath comes back around again, only this time, God is extending Sabbath beyond a weekly rest; it is a rhythm for how the entire community functions. Each week the servants and strangers to the nation are to share in the Sabbath rest, and there is even provision for their land to have a year of rest.

Through these laws, God is calling the people to holiness and showing them what it looks like to live holy lives. He commands them to be different from the other nations. He also reminds them that He is the source of their freedom and that freedom should cause them to live differently.

After these laws, God presents a promise. In Exodus 23:20-32, what promise does God give the people?

More often than not, God's call or command is partnered with a promise. Here at the base of Sinai, God assures Israel that they are headed into the land He promised to Abraham. He lets them know that they will take possession of the land that is currently inhabited by other nations. He promises to drive them out and bless them richly in the land. But God partners a warning with this promise.

What does God warn Israel not to do when they enter the land?

When the long list of laws is broken down, the commands are simple: Love your neighbor well and love God alone. Do not serve the gods of other nations. Destroy their idols and alters. Do not enter into a covenant with those gods. Kick them out completely. Israel is not to allow anything to stay in the land or their community that will need their hearts astray.

This is the heart of the Law and the heart of our God. He is a God of love and that love is shown in justice, fairness, grace, and provision. He cares for people, and He is teaching Israel how to care for people in the same way.

WEEK FOUR

How does viewing the Law through the lens of God's love change how you read the sections about the Law?

Are there any idols in your life that are keeping you from loving God alone? Confess them and get rid of them.

After reading through the laws about loving neighbors, how does this change your view of what it looks like to love people? Are there any steps you need to take to restore, build, mend, or invest in a relationship with someone?

Day 25: What the Lord Requires

MEDITATE ON MICAH 6:8

Sometimes we overcomplicate the way God wants us to live. We get caught up in the *should* and *should nots*. We frantically try to discern what it is God would have us do next, but God has already told us what is right and what is required of us. Today's Scripture meditation helps us get back to the basics of what God asks of us. Sometimes simplifying is what is required to help us make our next step forward in faith and in love.

Prepare: Be still before the Lord. Ask Him to prepare your heart to read and engage with this Scripture. Lay your heart open before Him and ask Him to speak.

Read the Word: Read the passage slowly. What words or phrases stand out to you?

Meditate on the Word: Read the passage again. How does this word or phrase connect to your life?

Respond to the Word: Read the passage again. Be honest with God about your response to this word and passage. How do you feel about it? What are you thinking? How are you responding to God? How is God inviting you to respond?

Rest in the Word: Read the passage one more time. Simply rest in God's Word. Submit yourself to His presence and just be present with Him.

Live the Word: How will you live into what you read and heard today?

Day 26: Covenant Celebration

STUDY EXODUS 24-26

I'm a sucker for a wedding, especially if I'm good friends with both the bride and the groom. I get teary every time the groom spots his bride at the other end of the white runner. The vows find a weighty place in my heart, and I lend my support to these friends committing to a life of love, then I sigh longingly and clap enthusiastically when the couple seals their commitment with a kiss. And then, of course, I stuff myself with yummy food and dance the night away at the reception!

Weddings are wonderful, and really, there is something about Israel's experience at Sinai that feels kind of like a wedding. God and Israel have entered into a covenant together. God has taken this worn down group of slaves and He has married them to Himself. Like a contract, both parties promise to uphold their side of the commitment, then they celebrate that commitment. God has promised Israel abundance, rest, and a good life in a new home He has prepared for them. All He asks is for their trust and faithfulness. Israel agrees to those terms.

How does viewing this experience at Sinai as a wedding add to your understanding or appreciation of these last several chapters?

For the last few chapters, we've been watching and listening in as Moses delivers God's words to the people. The Ten Commandments and some more detailed laws have been presented to the people. Moses records the Law and sets up a monument—a physical reminder of Israel's commitment—and they present their sacrifices to the Lord. The Law is read again before the people and they commit again to God's covenant. This covenant ceremony finishes when Moses and some of the other leaders of Israel meet with God partway up the mountain and enjoy a feast.

What special event do the leaders experience on the mountain?

It is unclear what it means for the leaders to see God while up on the mountain, but it is obvious that this encounter with the Lord is a special one. Whether through a vision or viewing a partial piece of God, they catch a glimpse of the One they and their community have entered into covenant with, and I'm certain that experience impacted all of them deeply.

Once the festivities are completed, Moses is called back up the mountain alone because God has more instructions to give him. Leaving Aaron in charge, Moses trudges up the mountain for a forty-day chat with God to get instructions for the Tabernacle. The Tabernacle is to function as a mobile temple. Every aspect of the structure and the elements of worship are detailed here, and while it can be kind of tedious to read, these instructions are included for a reason. Let's look beneath the words themselves and get to the heart of things.

God is establishing His place among the people of Israel. Since they first set foot out of Egypt, He has been reshaping them as His own people.

WEEK FOUR

Israel has already covered a lot of ground in their relationship with God. Trust, provision, and holiness have all been lessons that have marked their understanding of God. Now, with the instructions about the Tabernacle, it is time for Israel to learn about another aspect of their relationship with God—worship.

I've been saying it since we reached the base of the mountain—God knows how this world is meant to function. We are wired for abundant and restful freedom, and at the heart of such freedom is worship.

When we are secure in who we are and confident in who God is, when we believe Him and trust Him, the next step is worship.

God is in this for the long game. He has pledged Himself to these people and He is giving them the means to be in relationship with Him. From the Ark of the Covenant to the Bread of the Presence, the lampstand and the Tabernacle structure itself, God is giving Israel a very physical way to worship, and He's being so detailed about it because they have not known worship like this before. In Egypt, there were multiple gods and temples. Depending on what a worshiper needed, they would go through rituals and offer sacrifices in hopes of appeasing the gods and getting what they wanted. That kind of worship was marked by desperation, debauchery, and the fickleness of Egypt's gods. If the people gave enough of themselves, maybe their god would listen.

That is not the kind of worship we find at Sinai. Every piece of the Tabernacle is a reminder of God's presence among His people and His covenant with them. When they come to worship, they are to come humbly, trusting the God who brought them out of Egypt. The whole goal here is for God to dwell among His people. They don't have to go out and find Him or wonder if He's with them. His presence will rest right among them, right in the center of their camp.

How are you making space for God in your life? As modern-day Christians, we don't need to enter a place of worship in order to encounter God, but how are you making space for Him in your heart, life, and schedule? What can you do to make more space for Him?

Day 27: Your Body, His Temple

MEDITATE ON 1 CORINTHIANS 6:19-20

When the Holy Spirit came, He eliminated the need for us to meet with God in physical buildings. Instead, our bodies became His dwelling place. In today's Scripture meditation, we're going to focus on what it looks like for God's Spirit to dwell in us, for our lives to be His Tabernacle.

Prepare: Be still before the Lord. Ask Him to prepare your heart to read and engage with this Scripture. Lay your heart open before Him and ask Him to speak.

Read the Word: Read the passage slowly. What words or phrases stand out to you?

Meditate on the Word: Read the passage again. How does this word or phrase connect to your life?

Respond to the Word: Read the passage again. Be honest with God about your response to this word and passage. How do you feel about it? What are you thinking? How are you responding to God? How is God inviting you to respond?

Rest in the Word: Read the passage one more time. Simply rest in God's Word. Submit yourself to His presence and just be present with Him.

Live the Word: How will you live into what you read and heard today?

Day 28: Riding the Rhythm of Rest

SABBATH

....

I've noticed a pattern on my Sabbath days. As I finish my work and surrender my time and burdens to the Lord, it inevitably creates a little extra space, not only in my calendar, but also in my heart and mind. All that extra space has often resulted in two things: anxiety and inspiration.

It has happened almost every week for the last several weeks. I wake up on Saturday morning with a moment of peace, enjoying the realization that I have the day off, but then the panic sets in and I wonder how I'm going to spend my day and fill my time. I'll tell you right now, that is not a normal Sabbath response. Okay, well it is normal for us humans who are learning how to rest, but it isn't the response God intends for us to have on our day off.

I am a type-A person driven by accomplishments and the completion of tasks. I fill my time with checklists and to-do lists and often find my sense of worth in what I do—which isn't exactly a healthy thing. So when I wake up on the Sabbath, my brain rushes to figure out how I can accomplish something on a day that is not meant for accomplishing anything. I also tend to freak out about spending my day the wrong way. What if the things I choose to spend my time on don't fill me up or don't help me rest? What if I come to the end of Sabbath more tired than when I started it?

Embracing Sabbath is going to bring a lot of junk to the surface. Perhaps you've already experienced that in the three weeks we've been practicing together. Sabbath clears out the noise and leaves us with God and ourselves and all those internal things we've been avoiding. And sometimes, when those things rise up on Sabbath, we need to sit with them for a while. We don't need to try to fix ourselves or hide from our emotions or identity issues. Instead, we welcome them, give them space, and surrender them to the Lord from a place of rest.

On those mornings when I wake in a panic, I've learned to name my feelings and let the thoughts run their course as I surrender them to the Lord. I remind myself—and ask God to remind me—about the purpose of Sabbath. The point is resting and enjoying the day, and if to do that I need to give my soul a bit of attention, well, that's part of Sabbath too. It is more restful to confront those feelings rising up inside me than to try to outrun them. Instead of hiding from my emotions, I engage with them and embrace them. I take time to listen to what's going on inside me and allow my emotions to be another way to engage with God. By giving my emotions attention, I actually find myself better able to rest.

I also notice on Sabbath days, usually when I'm in the middle of reading my Bible, ideas will come to mind. Things I want to do, Bible studies I want to write, products, projects, or purchases that matter to me. I used to push all of that stuff away and anxiously try to outrun it or hide it so that I could rest, but I've learned, much like following the thought thread of my Sabbath anxiety and giving my emotions space to air out, to just let the thoughts come. I grab a notepad and a pen and jot everything down until my mind calms and I return to rest.

Resting often leads to inspiration and new ideas, and that's a good thing. I heard someone describe rest as doing the thing that makes you feel most like you. If those ideas and inspirations have anything to do with a craft project, a painting, or something creative, I'll act on them. I'll give myself space to gather up supplies and make something with my hands. If those ideas are work related, I simply write them down and save them for later when it's time to work again.

During your Sabbath practice, there will be times when things come up. Emotions will rise to the surface that you didn't know you had. The day will be interrupted by something that truly does need your immediate attention. Inspiration will strike and you'll have a great idea or dream you want to pursue. Make space to acknowledge those things and bring them before the Lord. Allow those things to be avenues to experience God's presence. Give yourself the space and time to just be with yourself. Surrender any expectations of what you think your Sabbath day should be. Sabbath is a gift for us, not another thing for us to control. Do not beat yourself up for not having a perfect Sabbath. There is no such thing. Sabbath takes practice and each Sabbath day is a little—and sometimes a lot—different. The goal is to surrender ourselves to whatever the day holds and allow each experience to connect us with God and rest in who He is and what He says about you.

SABBATH REFLECTION

How was your Sabbath practice this week?

What things have you noticed coming up on the Sabbath? Distractions? Disruptions? Emotions? Ideas? Jot them down.

How are you responding when those things come up?

FINALLY FREE

How can you continue to surrender these things to the Lord and use them as connecting points with Him?

Week Five

Day 29: Redemption Story

STUDY EXODUS 27-29

Every week at my home church, we close Sunday service by reciting what we call our "New Life Blessing." It is a benediction we speak over each other and it ends with these words: "We are blessed so that we can bless others. We are very blessed."

Those lines aren't original. They come from the words God spoke to Abraham in Genesis 12:2 when He promised Abraham land and descendants. Blessing is Israel's heritage and their legacy.

Israel was blessed so that they would be a blessing.

Through this one family, God would redeem the entire world from sin and death, and He would restore the relationship between Him and humanity that had been broken by sin. This redemption story found its beginning in the willingness of one man to follow God into a new land and trust Him for a seemingly crazy promise, but the next chapter of redemption begins here at Sinai.

FINALLY FREE

Everything at this mountain has deeper meaning. We can look with our modern-day lens and just see a list of rules and expectations that seem far too difficult to follow. We can mindlessly read the detailed instructions for the Tabernacle and the consecration of the priests and wonder how this applies to us. But everything God does has a meaning attached to it—often several layers of meaning.

On this side of the story, we have the benefit of several more generations of history after Israel's year at Mount Sinai. Since the Bible is one continuous story of God's love and redemption, we're going to dig into those deeper layers of meaning and tug on some threads that lead us to Jesus—the ultimate fulfillment of God's promise to Abraham, and the climax of God's redemption story.

When we read the genealogy of Moses and Aaron back in Exodus 6, I mentioned that when you read more monotonous passages like genealogies, it is helpful to notice the pattern and pay attention to when that pattern is broken. The same kind of reading can help us when we are reading sections of the Law. Between the instructions for the Tabernacle and priestly garments, there are a few places where the pattern of instruction is broken up with a bit of narrative or repetition for the sake of emphasis. Maybe you noticed those while you were reading today. Those breaks in pattern in today's chapters all revolve around Aaron as priest.

Take another look at Exodus 27:20-21. These two verses detail the use of the lampstand we read about a few chapters back. What instructions about this lampstand catch your attention?

Light is a common theme throughout the Bible. It is the first act of Creation and one of the names attributed to Jesus (John 8:12). In the plans for the Tabernacle, Moses is instructed to keep the lampstand continuously lit. Aaron and his sons, as priests, are to make sure the lampstand always has oil in it and that it stays burning. The Israelites are also to help keep the lamp burning with their sacrifices of pure olive oil that will be used as fuel.

Like a moth, I'm drawn to this idea of light. It served a practical purpose, I'm sure, so that the priests could do their work. But I also like the symbolism of it. Like so many other articles in the Tabernacle, the constant light of the lampstand is a reminder of God's constant presence and light among His people. It is a symbol of the light of God's Law that breaks through the darkness and illuminates the freedom of His presence and redemption. The lamp must always remain lit, for God is always with His people.

Further down in the passage there is another break in the instructions given about the priestly garments, specifically when God describes the breast piece Aaron is to wear as High Priest. This article of the priestly garment holds precious stones with the names of the tribes of Israel engraved on each stone.

In Exodus 28:29-30, God provides a bit of narrative about this particular garment and repeats a phrase. What is the phrase and why do you think God repeats it?

Aaron's role as priest isn't just about the tasks assigned to him. As High Priest, Aaron represents the people before God. When he comes before the Lord, as he seeks direction and makes decisions, the breast piece is to be a reminder for Aaron to carry the people of Israel in his heart. With all that gold and all those stones, I imagine that element of his garments has some weight to it, and I'm sure that is intentional. The role of priest is not one to be taken lightly. His job is to help the people atone for their sins, to call them toward holiness, and to lead them in worship. Every time Aaron wears the breast piece, it is a weighty reminder of the people—his people—whom he carries in his heart.

In the same way, centuries later, we see Jesus stepping in to fill that role. He becomes our new High Priest who carries our names on His heart and represents us before the Father. The book of Hebrews clearly presents this picture of Jesus as our High Priest, and establishes that His priesthood is different, better, and complete, whereas the priesthood established here in Exodus is just a shadow of things to come.

Read the following three passages in Hebrews. How do they describe Jesus' role as High Priest?

Hebrews 4:14-16

Hebrews 5:1-10

Hebrews 8:1-6

While the Tabernacle and the priests definitely serve a purpose in the new nation of Israel, they also give us hints of something—or rather, Someone—greater that is coming. That's not to disregard the work God is doing at Sinai. It is another step in God's redemption plan. As readers on this side of history, we can approach this narrative with Jesus in mind. Aaron will not be the perfect priest. He is human and flawed, and very soon in our Exodus narrative, those flaws will be apparent. But Jesus is the perfect High Priest. He goes before the Father holy and blameless. He represents us and carries us over His heart. Once and for all, Jesus bore our guilt and sin, and victoriously brought about our salvation.

While Aaron and the priesthood did not permanently solve Israel's sin and disobedience problem—they still had to make regular sacrifices until Jesus came and gave His live for us—the laws and sacrificial system made the people aware of their sin and shortcomings as well as their need for God. Ultimately, that's what the book of Exodus is all about—our need for God. We can't find freedom on our own. We don't know what it looks like and we certainly can't get to that place without Him. God used Israel as a model of what redemption and freedom looks like, and at the core it looks like living in relationship with God.

That has been God's goal all along—relationship:

I will dwell among the Israelites and be their God. And they will know that I am the LORD their God, who brought them out of the land of Egypt, so that I might dwell among them. I am the LORD their God (Exodus 29:45-46).

His desire is to be among His people. For Israel, He creates plans for a Tabernacle. Later, He will send His only Son to die on a cross and rise again on the third day. This Son will take up His position as High Priest and give us the gift of His Spirit to reside within in our hearts. In the New Covenant under Jesus, we become walking Tabernacles for the Lord, bearing His light to this dark world, and living free as His beloved people.

How does the Law come alive for you when you read it with Jesus in mind?

How can you carry God's light, love, and redemption story to someone who desperately needs the kind of freedom only found in Christ?

Day 30: Light and Salt

MEDITATE ON MATTHEW 5:13-16

In the Tabernacle, the lampstand was to burn continuously, a beacon of hope and light to those walking in darkness. Today, Jesus has put His Spirit in us so that we can be His light in the world. In today's Scripture meditation, we're going to settle into the idea of what it means to be Jesus' light and learn what it looks like to shine brightly for Him.

Prepare: Be still before the Lord. Ask Him to prepare your heart to read and engage with Scripture. Lay your heart open before Him and ask Him to speak.

Read the Word: Read the passage slowly. What words or phrases stand out to you?

Meditate on the Word: Read the passage again. How does this word or phrase connect to your life?

Respond to the Word: Read the passage again. Be honest with God about your response to this word and passage. How do you feel about it? What are you thinking? How are you responding to God? How is God inviting you to respond?

Rest in the Word: Read the passage one more time. Simply rest in God's Word. Submit yourself to His presence and just be present with Him.

Live the Word: How will you live into what you read and heard today?

Day 31: A People Set Apart

STUDY EXODUS 30-31

Have you been picking up on this theme of things being set apart? Throughout all of the instructions, there is this recurring requirement that each of these objects created for use in the Tabernacle is to be holy and set apart for God. They are not to have any other use than that which God has outlined.

The objects of worship aren't the only thing set apart, though. In Exodus 30:11-16, we also see God setting apart the people. Instructions for a census are given. Look again at the passage. Who is to participate in the census and what is this a sign of?

The people are to be counted, specifically, the men who are over twenty years old. This will be the group of people that will later go into battle when Israel claims the Promised Land. These men are to be set apart and numbered, and as part of their set-apartness, they are to pay a half-shekel, which acts as both an offering to the Lord and a ransom for their lives. Every step of the way as He delivers the Law, God is continuing to remind His people that He is their strength and their security. He is their source of life and salvation.

We also find two men in particular whom God has chosen and consecrated: Bezalel and Oholiab. With all the instructions God gave Moses about how the Tabernacle and its various elements are to be constructed, He has also raised up two men who are skilled enough to bring the Tabernacle to life. Not only that, but God says that He has "put wisdom in the heart of every skilled artisan in order to make all that I have commanded" (verse 6). He hasn't asked them to do the impossible. Israel has all of the supplies they need because of the generosity of the Egyptians when Israel left Egypt. They have skilled men who can lead the people in creating everything, and they have their God who is very intimately involved in the entire process.

People aren't the only ones being set apart. At the end of Exodus 31, we loop back to Sabbath, the one day a week that is set apart as holy to the Lord. In the English Standard Version, when the Lord delivers instructions about what Moses is to say to the people about Sabbath, verse 12 says, "Above all you shall keep my Sabbaths, for this is a sign between me and you throughout your generations, that you may know that I, the Lord, sanctify you."

"Above all" is an interesting phrase here. Israel has received the Ten Commandments and some other instructions about how people are to be treated in their community. Yet, Sabbath is the thing that is to be practiced "above all." Those who do not obey God's established boundaries of Sabbath will face dire consequences.

Why? Why put so much emphasis on this day of rest?

We've already talked about a few of those reasons in our study. What are some of the reasons you remember? (Flip back through our earlier lessons if you need a quick refresher.)

WEEK FIVE

Sabbath was meant to be a defining mark, setting Israel apart from the other nations. It was also meant to be a refining rhythm. Sabbath reminds us where our true worth and identity lies. It reminds us that we do not earn our own salvation. God is our Savior and provider. He is the One who makes us holy and no amount of trying or working or striving can accomplish that for us.

It was unheard of in other cultures to have regular and extended periods of time when the entire community rested from their work. Resting from work during festivals was a common practice, but a weekly day off was quite unusual. Israel knows this well, having just spent the last few generations in the grip of Pharaoh's ever-demanding rule. While death may seem like an extreme consequence for breaking Sabbath, God is re-establishing the focus of this nation and rest is an essential part of their new life.

While we aren't bound by the same laws and consequences—there is no rule to say Christians must practice Sabbath—it is a rhythm that is good for our souls. Like Israel, we need to let go of our own ideas of what freedom and abundance look like and receive God's way of doing things. He says rest is key and Sabbath is essential. It is the thing that sets us apart from others because we trust God enough to take a day off. Others may call it reckless, irresponsible, or even crazy, but Sabbath is one way of staking claim on our faith in the God who takes care of us. It is our way of saying that we won't give in to the rat race. We won't work ourselves into the grave and we can't work ourselves into grace. We will instead lean into this identity of being a set-apart people and find rest there.

How have things changed in your heart or life as you've been practicing Sabbath?

How has this idea of being set apart challenged or encouraged you today?

Day 32: Chosen People

MEDITATE ON 1 PETER 2:9-10

Israel was the first group of people God called and set apart for His purposes, but under Jesus, we too have become part of the family. God has called us, chosen us, and set us apart to share the hope of Jesus with the world. How we live matters. It matters for our own souls, but also for those who are watching and trying to figure out if this Jesus guy is worth trusting. In today's Scripture meditation, Peter lays out some very powerful words that define our identity as followers of Christ. Let these words encourage you to continue to live into that identity.

Prepare: Be still before the Lord. Ask Him to prepare your heart to read and engage with this Scripture. Lay your heart open before Him and ask Him to speak.

Read the Word: Read the passage slowly. What words or phrases stand out to you?

Meditate on the Word: Read the passage again. How does this word or phrase connect to your life?

Respond to the Word: Read the passage again. Be honest with God about your response to this word and passage. How do you feel about it? What are you thinking? How are you responding to God? How is God inviting you to respond?

Rest in the Word: Read the passage one more time. Simply rest in God's Word. Submit yourself to His presence and just be present with Him.

Live the Word: How will you live into what you read and heard today?

Day 33: The God of Justice and Compassion

STUDY EXODUS 32-33

It's been forty days since Moses climbed Mount Sinai to convene with God in that cloud. Forty days since the other leaders of Israel feasted on the mountain in God's presence. We've spent the last several chapters up on that mountain with Moses, listening in as God gave him instructions about the Law and the Tabernacle. Now let's climb back down and catch up with the people of Israel.

In short, things aren't going too well.

Moses has been gone too long and the people have grown impatient and perhaps a little bit scared that Moses isn't actually coming back down. Since Aaron is the one in charge in Moses' absence, the people come to him with a request.

FINALLY FREE

What did the people ask Aaron to do for them, and what is Aaron's response?

Even after all this time of walking with these people, I'm still pretty quick to judge them. It was one thing to doubt God's provision of water in the desert, but to ask Aaron to make gods for them after Moses has been gone a few weeks, especially after they heard God speak and witnessed the presence of His cloud on the mountain just seems crazy. I want to yell at them, "What do you think you're doing?!" But then I hear the voice of grace and remember that I'm not too much different from Israel. If I had gone through what they did, perhaps I would have responded similarly.

The leader who had been a physical reminder of God's presence among the Israelites is gone and they are afraid he isn't coming back. They're looking for something, anything to physically stake their faith on, so they fall back on what they know. They remember the Egyptian gods and temples and all of the statues and monuments the Egyptians used to worship, and they ask Aaron to make them one of those. And Aaron does. He has the people collect up the gold they had brought with them out of Egypt—the gold meant for the building of the Tabernacle and its various articles—and forms a golden calf for them.

In the past, I've read this passage to mean that Israel set up a brand new god to worship, but I'm not sure that's what's happening here. I don't think they're making a *new* god. They are making an *image* of God. This act of desperation causes a lot of trouble for them, though. Just a few short days ago, God had clearly stated that they were not to make any image of Him (Exodus 20:4). He wanted them to trust Him, not a cold, lifeless object.

While the people are partying and worshiping around this golden calf, God, aware of what the people are doing, instructs Moses to go down the mountain to the people. God's plan is to destroy the people for their disobedience and continue His covenant through Moses alone.

What fascinates me so much about these chapters is how Moses responds to God's plan. If you remember from earlier in our study, Moses wasn't too keen on God's plan to use Moses to free Israel from Egypt. The journey to Sinai wasn't easy either.

WEEK FIVE

Moses had to deal with the people's complaints and their distrust of God. Now, when he has the opportunity to be rid of the people, Moses calls upon God's compassion and faithfulness. He reminds God of how the Egyptians saw God's power when He brought Israel out, and he calls upon the covenant God made with Abraham, Isaac, and Jacob.

God is a God of justice, and sin must be dealt with. But He is also a God of compassion and grace, the One who is faithful and true. Moses calls upon the compassionate side of God's character and asks Him to be merciful to the people. When Moses comes down the mountain, however, and sees the extent of the people's sin, he is enraged and smashes the tablets with God's covenant engraved on them. Only a little over a month into this new way of life and the people have already broken faith with God.

How does Moses respond to the people's unfaithfulness?

While I was writing this lesson, I was discussing it with a seminary friend of mine and he pointed out something interesting. What happens in the camp as a result of the golden calf incident is like a second Passover. After destroying the idol and forcing those who participated in idol worship to drink the water with the ground up gold from the statue, Moses sends the Levites to pass through the camp and kill those who had been unfaithful. Not everyone dies. The nation remains, but those who have been unfaithful face God's judgement.

It feels harsh. Thirty thousand lives were lost that day, and that is sometimes what makes the Old Testament hard to read. It is much easier to see God's wrath and judgment than His love and grace here.

While the consequences for Israel's actions may seem harsh, the penalty for sin is death. There is no way to tiptoe around that fact. The rest of Scripture and the rest of the Law lays out a foundation for how to deal with sin in community. The reality is, God has outlined what is required of the people, and the people agreed. They chose this new covenant of faithfulness to God. They received the Ten Commandments when God spoke them to the people, but Israel let their distrust overtake them when

Moses stayed too long on the mountain. They needed something visible to rest their faith on, so they worshiped the calf instead of trusting the invisible God who had been leading them all along in visible ways.

What visible proof did God give Israel to let them know He was with them?

One thing fascinates me, though. From my human perspective, while the people certainly were in the wrong, Aaron doesn't seem to be punished for his role in the whole thing. He didn't worship the calf, from what I can gather from the text, but he did create the thing. It seems like he should at least get a reprimand or something. I've sat here and pondered it for a while, and all I can think of is that Aaron not being numbered among those who died that day is an act of great grace.

A lot of people died and even more ended up sick because of a plague, but Aaron was not one of them. For whatever reason—because he wasn't one of the worshipers or because of the simple and profound grace of God—Aaron lived and fought alongside his brothers to purge Israel's camp.

How does the grace offered to Aaron encourage you?

Once the people have been dealt with, Moses goes back up the mountain to appeal to God's kindness. He even goes so far as to say that if God isn't willing to forgive the people, Moses will offer himself up for punishment in the Israel's place (Exodus 32:32). I think this is another appeal to God's character. Moses knows God to be merciful, so he is asking God to show mercy. And God does. The people are still accountable for their sins, but God is not going to follow through on His plan to start over with Moses and He is not going to remove His presence from among Israel. In fact, He does the opposite and comes closer to the people. In the very next chapter, the Tent of Meeting is set up outside of the camp. Moses isn't going up the mountain

WEEK FIVE

to meet with God for weeks at a time anymore. Instead, the people watch him walk to the outskirts of the camp and meet with God there.

For the entirety of this study, we've been reading Exodus with the lens of freedom. We've been looking to understand what this freedom is that God wants to give us, and we've unearthed a lot of truth so far. But maybe you're struggling to see that freedom theme in these chapters. Israel made some bad choices and they suffered the consequences for it. Where is the freedom in that?

Perhaps freedom is found, not in Israel's actions, but in Moses'. I think he is our glimpse of freedom here, because in Moses, all I can see is Jesus. Like Moses, Jesus is the one going to the Father on our behalf. Jesus is the one stepping in to take care of our sin problem. Jesus is the one restoring relationship between us and God when we have broken faith with Him.

Jesus is our abundance.

Jesus is our rest.

Jesus is our freedom.

And while in Scripture, Jesus won't make His earthly appearance until generations later, we see whispers and hints of Him here.

Are there any other ways you see abundance, rest, or freedom in this difficult passage?

Is there any sin hindering your relationship with God that you need to confess now? Lean into His grace and seek His mercy.

Day 34: Trusting the Shepherd

MEDITATE ON PSALM 23

Throughout Exodus we see Moses acting as a shepherd to the people of Israel. This image of the shepherd is another one that Moses and Jesus share. In today's Scripture meditation, we're going to explore this idea of Jesus as our shepherd and the freedom, abundance, and rest He provides as we entrust ourselves to His care.

Prepare: Be still before the Lord. Ask Him to prepare your heart to read and engage with this Scripture. Lay your heart open before Him and ask Him to speak.

Read the Word: Read the passage slowly. What words or phrases stand out to you?

Meditate on the Word: Read the passage again. How does this word or phrase connect to your life?

Respond to the Word: Read the passage again. Be honest with God about your response to this word and passage. How do you feel about it? What are you thinking? How are you responding to God? How is God inviting you to respond?

Rest in the Word: Read the passage one more time. Simply rest in God's Word. Submit yourself to His presence and just be present with Him.

Live the Word: How will you live into what you read and heard today?

Day 35: Connect in Community and Enjoy Creation

SABBATH

One of the things that can make Sabbath challenging is some of the preconceived notions about this scheduled day of rest. Sometimes when the idea of Sabbath is presented it is done with a long list of what we cannot do. When that happens, Sabbath feels more stifling and confining instead of freeing and restful. We can become so focused on what we're "not allowed to do" that we miss out on the enjoyment Sabbath is meant to bring.

I reached the point in my own Sabbath practice where Sabbath felt more like a burden. I was trying to stay away from technology, from planning things, from errands, and chores. Aside from lying in bed and reading a book, though, I didn't know how to spend my time. Around that time I felt the Lord invite me into something new. I felt Him challenging me to view Sabbath as a day for fun. He encouraged me to throw out the perceived rules I thought I needed to follow and just focus on letting my Sabbath be fun. I was hesitant about the idea, but decided to give it a try and began making space for the things I thought were fun—hanging out with a friend, treating myself to brunch, window shopping, wandering around a craft store, entertaining creative ideas, indulging in a book, enjoying a movie or show, working on a passion project. As I let Sabbath become a space for fun, I found myself looking forward to my practice each week.

While Sabbath is a rhythm of rest, resting doesn't always mean napping or refraining from exerting any energy. It is true that physical rest is part of Sabbath, and we should listen to our bodies and give them rest. But our hearts, minds, and souls need rest too, and sometimes the most restful thing we can do is let go of responsibility for a bit and do something we enjoy doing just because we think it's fun. I've heard it said that if you spend time working with your brain during the week, spend Sabbath using your hands. The opposite is also true. If you work with your hands during the week, give your brain some space on Sabbath The point here is to engage in life-giving activities.

Sabbath also doesn't have to be practiced in isolation. In fact, it shouldn't be. Throughout the book of Exodus, as God continues to cycle back to the commands about Sabbath, those commands are given in the context of community. Sabbath is a communal practice where we rest and enjoy together. It is a time for connecting with loved ones, sharing a meal, and enjoying time together.

If your Sabbath practice has felt a little less than restful or if you have felt the burden of how to fill your time, consider adding in some time for relationship and fun.

SABBATH REFLECTION

Have you settled into a rhythm of consistent Sabbath yet? If not, what is keeping you from doing that?

WEEK FIVE

Who are some people in your life that you enjoy spending time with? How might you invite them into your Sabbath rhythm?

What activities or hobbies do you find enjoyable and restful? How might you add those into your Sabbath rhythm?

Week Six

Day 36: The God of Grace and Rest

STUDY EXODUS 34-35

After the golden calf incident, what happens in today's passage is nothing but grace. It's almost like God hit the rewind button and reset everything back to before Israel broke covenant. God re-establishes boundaries around the mountain and calls Moses up to meet with Him. He gives Moses the Ten Commandments on a new set of tablets and reviews important elements of the Law and His expectations for Israel.

It almost feels like the whole calf-thing never happened, and in some ways, I want that to be true. I want to act like Israel never worshiped that idol, but I think this passage and God's grace is even more rich and abundant because God still extends relationship to Israel.

Up on the mountain in Exodus 34:5-9, God reveals His name and His nature. What do we learn about Him and His character? What kind of God is He?

We remember what happened at the base of the mountain with the idol. We saw the devastation Israel's sin caused in their community. We saw their repentant hearts, and we heard God's conversation with Moses when Moses called on God's faithfulness and love. Here in these early verses of Exodus 34, we see God making a declaration about His character. He is both kind and just, loving and generous. He deals with sin, but He also deals in love and grace.

With this self-declaration from God, Moses intercedes once more on behalf of Israel, asking God to go with them and claim them as His possession, His chosen people. Moses refuses to move forward alone, and God agrees. He reaffirms His covenant with Israel and establishes Himself as a jealous God—not one who is envious, but one who is concerned for the well-being of His people—and He commands Israel not to give in to the customs of the foreign nations whose land they are about to claim. They are to get rid of the idols and elements of worship in any land they take. Those things have no place among God's people. Israel is also not to intermarry with the people of the land, lest their spouses lead them astray.

It's at this point where God reviews some essential pieces of the Law. Look at the laws God reminds the people of. Many of these have shown up more than once. What do you think is the significance of these particular laws and what is the purpose of repeating them?

While this collection of laws may seem random and disconnected, when I look at them, I see a God who is reminding His people of who He is and who they are. They are a people who worship one God and one God alone. They are a people who are not defined by their work, but by rest, celebration, and the assurance that their God will take care of them. They are a people who remember what God has done for them, and their previous experience with God's faithfulness feeds their present faith.

Like the first time this covenant was established, Moses spends forty days and forty nights up on the mountain, communing with God, and this time, when he returns to the people, he doesn't find them worshiping idols. They are waiting and ready to hear the word of the Lord. When instructions are given for the people to collect an offering for the building of the Tabernacle, they do so generously. Everyone gives according to what they can, whether materials or skills, and the creation of the Tabernacle begins. No longer will He dwell outside the camp in the Tent of Meeting, or up on the mountain. Very soon God's presence will settle right in the midst of His people.

How does the beginning of the Tabernacle further reveal God's grace to you?

There are times in our lives when we may feel like the choices we've made have forever separated us from God. We may feel our actions are irredeemable, that God would never welcome us back, but Israel's story tells us otherwise.

The golden calf isn't the last time Israel will go astray from God or choose something else over Him. This isn't the last time they will run after something physical when God has asked them to trust what they cannot see. But this is also not the last time God will extend His kindness, compassion, and grace to the people.

God can't live among sin. Sin will always separate us from God, but we serve a God who goes to great lengths to get us back, to make a way for us to lay sin aside and live in His grace. Here on this re-do at Mount Sinai, that grace cannot be more apparent.

In His grace, God reminds the people to rest.

Do not worship idols; *rest* in God's invisible presence.

Do not work yourselves to the bone; take a day off each week and enjoy *rest*.

Do not put long hours in at the field during harvest and planting seasons; *rest* and trust the Lord to take care of your crops.

Rest in the goodness of the Lord who gives grace and love.

Rest in the justice of the Lord who deals with sin and makes a way for us to be with Him.

Rest in the presence of the Lord who is present among His people.

Rest and find freedom in His arms of grace.

How do you feel about God after reading His interactions with Israel after everything that happened with the Golden Calf?

How might you lean into the truth of who God is? Read Exodus 34:5-9 again. Which aspect of God's character do you need to press into today?

At the end of this lesson we listed a lot of different ways God invited Israel to rest. Do any of those ways resonate with the kind of rest you need in this season?

Day 37: Know that He is God

MEDITATE ON PSALM 46

After experiencing God's grace and forgiveness for their idol worship, Israel enters a new phase of their relationship with God. They've been in relationship for a while now, continuing to learn about who He is and how to trust Him. With the advent of this re-do covenant, Israel is sure of their position as His people. If we're going to find freedom, we need to be sure of who God is. In today's Scripture meditation, we'll explore that very thing, and like Israel, I hope this passage leads you into a deeper trust and understanding of the God you've chosen to follow.

Prepare: Be still before the Lord. Ask Him to prepare your heart to read and engage with this Scripture. Lay your heart open before Him and ask Him to speak.

Read the Word: Read the passage slowly. What words or phrases stand out to you?

Meditate on the Word: Read the passage again. How does this word or phrase connect to your life?

Respond to the Word: Read the passage again. Be honest with God about your response to this word and passage. How do you feel about it? What are you thinking? How are you responding to God? How is God inviting you to respond?

Rest in the Word: Read the passage one more time. Simply rest in God's Word. Submit yourself to His presence and just be present with Him.

Live the Word: How will you live into what you read and heard today?

Day 38: The Generosity of Forgiveness

STUDY EXODUS 36-37

On first read, today's passage at the tail end of Exodus feels like notes for a building project. They also feel a little repetitive from when the building instructions were given to Moses on the mountain. It makes me wonder why the author recorded the account of the building of the Tabernacle in this way. Why go through the trouble of writing out each and every detail of the building process? Why not just say, "And Israel built the Tabernacle and all of its instruments of worship as the Lord instructed"? That would have saved the author a lot of time and words.

Maybe you've found yourself asking similar questions of today's passage. If so, that's great! Those kinds of questions are what help us make the move from simply reading the Bible to studying it. We're digging deep, looking between the lines, putting ourselves in the shoes—or sandals—of our author and the people in these chapters.

Why do you think the author included the details about everything that was built and how it was built?

Exodus is a historical book and one of five key books that make up the Pentateuch, a central piece of the Jewish Scriptures. The author obviously thought it was important to include all the building details here. In order to get a better understanding of this passage, let's look at the larger context it appears in.

Since arriving at the base of Mount Sinai in Exodus 19, what big events or conversations have happened up to this point? Feel free to consult our previous lessons to list as many things as you can.

Sinai is the place where God entered into a covenant with His people. It is also the place where He established the Law and provided instructions for their place of worship. The majority of this section of Exodus has mainly been about Moses receiving words from the Lord and passing them onto the people, then interceding on behalf of the people when they broke covenant with God.

WEEK SIX

Truthfully, Israel hasn't had much to do at Sinai until now. They have received God's words through Moses and witnessed His presence on the mountain, but their newfound faith and relationship with God hasn't had much action behind it. They've been waiting. Now in today's passage, it's time to move. It's time to get to work and bring about all of the instructions God gave Moses about the Tabernacle. The people give their offerings of materials for the building project, and they give generously. In fact, the people give so abundantly that the leaders of the building project approach Moses with an urgent request.

What do the leaders ask Moses to do? (See Exodus 36:2-6)

There is something so redemptive about these chapters. After everything that happened with the golden calf, to see Israel giving so generously and providing more than enough supplies that Moses has to ask the people to stop giving, it seems like nothing short of grace. The people have recommitted to God and they are all in. They are finally getting to act on the covenant and give to or help build the Tabernacle that will be a home for God's presence among His people. While the details of the building process may seem monotonous, each detail declares the people's obedience and faithfulness to God's commands. They are making a space for Him. They were disobedient in the past, but God gave them another chance to be faithful, and this time they follow through.

This passage declares the abundance of gratitude the people feel as they give their offerings, and the abundance of God to forgive and still live among His people. Perhaps that is why Israel gives so generously, because they have felt the weight of their sin. Their past choices aren't defining them. They are living into the grace and freedom that comes with God's forgiveness. Israel is modeling the words of Jesus when He told His disciples, "Freely you have received, freely give" (Matthew 10:8).

Part of the wonder of embracing the freedom we have in Christ is generously sharing that freedom with others. We don't hoard it or try to earn more of it—not that we could even if we tried. Instead, we give it away. We allow God's love, grace, and abundance to overflow from us and onto those who desperately need it. It's another way that this whole idea of being blessed so that we can bless others gets lived out.

Have you felt the weight of God's forgiveness? How has His grace enabled you to live freely and generously?

How can you be generous with the grace, love, and provision God has given you?

Day 39: Embracing the Gift of Forgiveness

MEDITATE ON 1 JOHN 1:5-9

One of the most amazing aspects of the Christian life is that, when we come to God and confess our sin, He forgives us completely. The slate is wiped clean and those habits, events, words, and actions that kept us from God before, no longer hinder us. We are forgiven and welcomed into relationship with God. In today's Scripture meditation, we're going to spend time reflecting on the forgiveness we have received from God, and embracing the freedom that comes with that great gift.

Prepare: Be still before the Lord. Ask Him to prepare your heart to read and engage with this Scripture. Lay your heart open before Him and ask Him to speak.

FINALLY FREE

Read the Word: Read the passage slowly. What words or phrases stand out to you?

Meditate on the Word: Read the passage again. How does this word or phrase connect to your life?

Respond to the Word: Read the passage again. Be honest with God about your response to this word and passage. How do you feel about it? What are you thinking? How are you responding to God? How is God inviting you to respond?

Rest in the Word: Read the passage one more time. Simply rest in God's Word. Submit yourself to His presence and just be present with Him.

Live the Word: How will you live into what you read and heard today?

Day 40: Finally Free

STUDY EXODUS 38-40

If you were to look back through the account of the building of the Tabernacle, you would find a phrase repeated at the end of every element that is built: "They made everything just as the Lord commanded Moses."

Go back through chapters 36-39 and underline every time that statement is made. How many times is this statement repeated?

Every element of the Tabernacle that is completed is a celebration of the faithful obedience of the people. In Exodus 39:32-43, that is the main focus as the finished

Tabernacle is brought to Moses for inspection. Moses sees that everything has been constructed according to the Lord's command, and he blesses the people. All that time at the base of Sinai, those difficult days when Israel wandered away from God, and His amazing redemption—all of that finds its climax here, as the Tabernacle is set up in the center of the camp.

A year after Israel arrived at Sinai, the center of their worship, their community, and their faith, has finally become a reality. The plans have been seen through to completion and the cloud symbolizing God's presence settles over the Tabernacle. If God's cloud stayed or moved on, Israel followed suit. They camped as long as God's presence rested over the Tabernacle, and if He moved, they packed up and moved with Him.

Israel is a different people than when they came out of Egypt. They have learned how to follow God, they have learned how to trust Him, and they are committed to doing life with Him. The narrative about following God's cloud feels like a happy conclusion for Israel's freedom story—one of those riding-off-into-the-sunset-to-live-happily-ever-after kind of moments. While their freedom has been established, their story is far from over. There is still the matter of the Promised Land they have yet to enter. All this time at Sinai has been preparation for that. There is also the matter of all the nations finding a blessing through Israel, and all nations experiencing the journey to freedom through Christ.

Yes, there is much more ahead for Israel. Their story will continue and they will make mistakes and wander from God, and God will continue to redeem and restore them. Yet, even knowing what's ahead for Israel, I don't think we can leave this study without acknowledging the work God has done here—in Israel, and in you and me.

How has this study of Exodus changed you and your understanding of God?

Before studying this Old Testament book, I had labeled it as a book of the Law that was interesting up to the point where Israel set up camp at Sinai. It was hard for me to see God's grace and love in all the commandments and in the plagues and signs God used to bring Israel out of Egypt. However, through these pages I have

WEEK SIX

learned to encounter a God who goes to incredible lengths to lead us into freedom. I've learned to notice God's grace even in the things that are hard, and I've accepted that, while His commands and laws may seem cumbersome, they are declarations about our identity as humans and constant reminders of our need for God.

But I think the most impactful thing about this study—and one of the most surprising things for me—is this thread of rest.

We are finally free when we press into the rhythms of rest God established and modeled when He created the world. Our God is not Pharaoh. He does not demand bricks and endless labor. He calls us to rest, to live in the abundance of His presence, to trust His provision and healing and care. Sabbath is a command to set Israel apart, and it is a lifestyle that we as New Covenant Christians are invited into.

Above all else, Exodus shows us the character of a God who fights for His people, rescues them out of the bondages that hold them captive, and ushers them into a new identity. When we are secure in who God is, we can rest in the freedom He gives us and we can live into our identity as His children, not His slaves.

As you finish this study, I pray you are able to see God's presence in your life and that you embrace the freedom He has already given you. Like Israel, I pray that you are able to follow His movements, receive His grace, and live in the freedom that is found in His presence.

In what ways has God set you free in this study?

How have the meditation and Sabbath practices helped you embrace the freedom and rest God gives you?

What's next? Is there a portion of this study He is inviting you to explore more deeply? Is there a passage of Scripture you want to meditate on further? Take time to ask God what comes next in your freedom journey.

Day 41: For Freedom We are Free

MEDITATE ON GALATIANS 5:1

It seems only fitting that our final Scripture meditation is spent in the verse that inspired this study. We can often fall into this idea that we are set free from sin in order to live a certain way for God. As we've seen throughout our study, there is a marked difference between how the people of God live compared to those who do not follow Him. We are meant to be set apart. But we are not freed so that we can enslave ourselves to a long list of expectations and rules. We are set free to live free. In today's Scripture meditation, we're going to focus on that idea and let that be the one we carry with us from this study.

Prepare: Be still before the Lord. Ask Him to prepare your heart to read and engage with this Scripture. Lay your heart open before Him and ask Him to speak.

Read the Word: Read the passage slowly. What words or phrases stand out to you?

Meditate on the Word: Read the passage again. How does this word or phrase connect to your life?

Respond to the Word: Read the passage again. Be honest with God about your response to this word and passage. How do you feel about it? What are you thinking? How are you responding to God? How is God inviting you to respond?

Rest in the Word: Read the passage one more time. Simply rest in God's Word. Submit yourself to His presence and just be present with Him.

Live the Word: How will you live into what you read and heard today?

Day 42: Overflowing from Rest

SABBATH

Sabbath isn't just a day of the week. It's a lifestyle. God commanded Israel to practice Sabbath, not just so they could have the day off, but so that they could engage with a soul habit of rest. A soul habit of rest is centered on the idea that God is good and He is good to us. This kind of rest is founded on the belief that God will take care of us and we can trust Him to do so. In this final Sabbath practice, we're going to let this Sabbath rhythm that we've spent the last six week's shaping overflow into every aspect of our lives.

The weekly rhythm of Sabbath is there to help us stop, reset, and rest, but Sabbath doesn't end at sundown on whatever day of the week we've chosen to practice. Sabbath is a lifestyle, a state of being, a way of existing. You may remember from our study that God continued to weave Sabbath rhythms into Israel's life and calendar even outside their weekly practice.

As we practice Sabbath, that rest we find on our day off is meant to define our entire week. When we allow Sabbath rest to overflow into the rest of the week, we carry with us that position of resting in God and trusting Him even while we work. We begin to view everything differently. Our work becomes an outflow of worship instead of endless toil to provide for our own needs. Our bills and financial struggles become places where we surrender to God's care and trust Him to provide. We no longer schedule our time with endless meetings and deadlines, but allow for some extra margin to give our bodies and souls time to rest every day.

While today marks the end of our time together, I hope you continue this Sabbath practice. Keep taking a day each week and set it aside to rest and enjoy God's presence. Keep preparing for Sabbath and surrendering to it. Find ways to connect with your community and have fun. As you do this, allow this rhythm of rest and the assurance of abundance in God's presence to overflow into your daily life.

Start from a place of rest instead of working in order to get to rest.

Stop treating rest as a reward for completed work and begin viewing rest as your starting place.

Listen to your body and your heart and give them the time they need during the week.

Live out of a place of believing that God is enough and He provides enough.

Trust Him to take care of you and stop striving.

Allow Sabbath to be a sign of the God's kingdom here on earth, a rhythm that sets you apart and one that God uses to make you more like Him.

If you're looking for ways to keep practicing these movements of Sabbath, you will find a resource called "Sabbath Movement Ideas" in the back of this book that can be used as a quick reference of everything we've talked about in our Sabbath practices.

A Note from Jazmin

Dear Heart,

You did it! You've reached the end of our journey through Exodus. I hope that you have experienced God in new ways and have learned how to better live into the freedom Christ has given you. I hope that the Bible has come to life for you in a new way and that this study has given you a new excitement for God's Word. I also hope that these devoted practices of reading Scripture intentionally, the weekly rhythm of Sabbath, and pausing to slowly meditate on Scripture have helped you learn how to live more devoted to God.

If this study has impacted you in any way, I would love to hear from you. You can connect with me on Facebook or Instagram @jazminnfrank or send me an email through the contact form on my website at jazminnfrank.com. My website is also a great place to learn more about how to love God, love His story, and live devoted. And if you're looking for your next Bible study to do yourself or with a group, don't forget to check out my other studies!

Live in His love!

Jazmin

How to Lead a Scripture Meditation for a Group

Since Scripture meditation is such an important aspect of *Finally Free,* I wanted to give you a bit of guidance for how to lead a scripture meditation practice in your small group. A couple of years ago, my small group began the practice of setting aside time to practice Scripture meditation together. About every quarter, and sometimes in between studies, we'll take a week to move through a practice. Meditating on Scripture independently is a good way to build our personal relationships with God, but there are also benefits to practicing in community. In addition to building relationship with God, meditating on Scripture in community is a great way to build relationship with each other. Meditating on Scripture as a group makes space for everyone to interact with God's Word, slow down, and listen to God.

If you're looking for a way to incorporate Scripture meditation into your small group, here are a few things to keep in mind:

PREPARE YOUR GROUP

Scripture meditation is a slow, reflective practice. It should not be rushed or crammed in at the end of a session. Dedicate an entire group session to this practice. Let your group members know ahead of time that you will be doing a Scripture meditation so they aren't caught off guard when they show up for group. Within each movement of the meditation there is space for reflection and sharing. Whether it's the first time or the twenty-fifth time your group has practiced together, it is also helpful before you begin to outline these five movements of the meditation.

1. *Read the Word:* The passage is read for the first time and everyone listens for a word or phrase that sticks out to them.

2. *Meditate on the Word:* The passage is read again and individuals are invited to reflect on the word or phrase that stuck out to them and meditate on why it matters to them.

3. *Respond to the Word:* The passage is read a third time and individuals take time to pray and respond to God, the word, and their own emotions related to the passage. They are also invited to ask God how He would have them respond to the passage.

4. *Rest in the Word:* The passage is read one final time, and the group simply listens and receives God's Word.

5. *Live the Word:* The group closes in prayer, each individual committing to keep living in relationship with God through what they received in the meditation practice.

KEEP THE PASSAGE SHORT

When it comes to picking a passage, keep it on the shorter side, usually 4-10 verses. It can also be helpful to give your readers the context of the passage they will be meditating on.

INVOLVE EVERYONE

When our group does a Scripture meditation, we have an established understanding that everyone shares. The only people who get a pass are guests who are visiting for the first time. In each movement of the meditation, after the passage is read and quiet time is given, ask each person to share. This will feel vulnerable and hard, but that's okay. Make sure you establish a safe space in the group for people to share. Scripture meditation has a way of sending us into hiding or striping away the walls we hide behind. We want to make sure that each group member feels supported and safe to share and engage with God in whatever way he or she needs to.

GO SLOW

From the reading, to the response time, to the space allotted for reflection, allow it all to progress slowly. Give everyone enough space to think, pray, reflect, and share. You've set the whole group time aside for this practice. There is no need to rush.

READ FROM MULTIPLE TRANSLATIONS

Since each movement of the Scripture meditation involves reading the same passage multiple times, I find it helpful to read from multiple translations. This is also another way to involve your group members. Rather than reading the passage each time yourself, ask your group members to read aloud from their translations. A different voice and a different translation may help individuals notice things they didn't in a previous reading.

Scripture meditation is a powerful tool to engage in God's Word as a community. I pray these tips help you lead your group through this practice and that all of you experience the power of God's Word and presence.

Sabbath Movement Ideas Chart

During a recent sermon series at my church on Sabbath, my friend Stephanie created a super helpful chart for the movements of Sabbath.[9] She refers to these as movements because Sabbath is not linear. Each movement overlaps with and plays into the others. She created this chart, not as a to-do list, but as a way to guide us in our Sabbath practice and provide ideas for how to engage in each movement. The days of Sabbath throughout this study are based on these ideas, and you can read more about each movement on Days 7, 14, 21, 28, 35, and 42. This resource is useful as a quick reference or as a way to get some more ideas for how to engage with God during Sabbath.

MOVEMENT #1: PREPARE

This is the movement that happens before the official Sabbath time. The purpose of this movement is to prepare the heart, mind, body, and space to rest with God.

Focus passage: Genesis 2:1-2

Ideas for engaging in this movement:

- Ask God to make you aware of His presence
- Clean the house
- Finish work and set it aside
- Grocery shopping
- Make a to-do list for Monday
- Touch base with others who are preparing for Sabbath

- Have kids finish work, homework, and chores
- Invite kids to pray for God to reveal Himself during Sabbath
- Get out any special Sabbath candles or foods
- Make sure animals are fed and settled in

MOVEMENT #2: SURRENDER

This movement begins Sabbath. In this movement, we remember that Sabbath is God's time and we surrender our time and our burdens to Him.

Focus passage: Exodus 20:8-11

Ideas for engaging in this movement:

- Light a candle
- Confess your sins
- Stop working
- Worship
- Practice Christian disciplines
- Read your Bible
- Don't schedule things on Sabbath
- Reschedule that thing you accidentally put on Sabbath
- Say NO
- Invite kids to talk about their week
- Invite kids to say how God was present this week
- Have a conversation about your week and how you saw God was present this week

MOVEMENT #3: CONNECT

This movement encourages community and communing with the Spirit. Use this movement to connect with God, others, and yourself.

Focus passage: Psalm 139

Ideas for engaging in this movement:

- Call a friend
- Meet up for a meal
- Host others for dinner
- Send kids to a friend's house or set up a playdate
- Go to a small group meeting
- Go on a date with your spouse
- Spend alone time with God
- Encourage kids to write, draw, or sing with Jesus
- Ask yourself, "How am I doing? What am I feeling?"
- Spend time alone with yourself

MOVEMENT #4: ENJOY

This movement invites you to embrace the fun, joy, and peace of Sabbath. Participate in the joy of new life in Christ and enjoy the freedom you have in Him.

Focus passage: Luke 4:16-21

Ideas for engaging in this movement:

- Do something you enjoy
- Eat good food
- Go for a hike
- Enjoy a museum
- Do some art
- Invite the kids to plan the day
- Take the dogs to the park
- Eat dessert first
- Bake something delicious
- Do a fun project
- Play a game with friends

- Surprise someone with a gift
- Visit a friend or family
- Read a good book
- Spend time on a hobby

MOVEMENT #5: OVERFLOW

This final movement is a reminder that Sabbath is a sign of the coming kingdom of God. It should overflow into our whole lives as we seek to live into Sabbath rest in some way every day.

Focus passage: Matthew 6:25-34

Ideas to engage with this movement:

- Take a lunch break
- Stop working at a reasonable time every day
- Don't stay late
- Let kids take a break before homework
- Slow down
- Eat dinner together
- Host others
- Take a vacation
- Buy yourself a present
- Don't work for work's sake
- Prioritize mental health and relationship before work
- Invite God to determine your schedule
- Make space for quiet, rest, and joy
- Embrace seasons of change and waiting

Devoted Scripture Journal

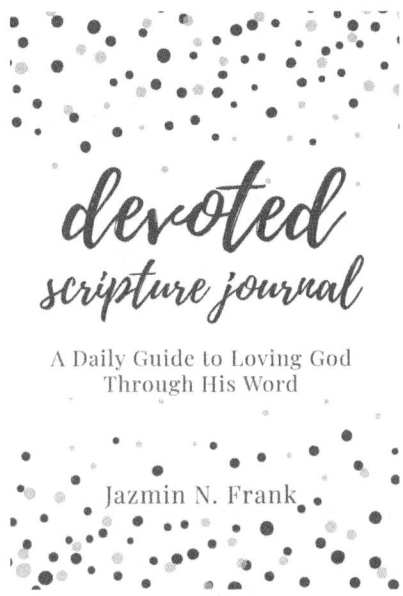

Take the next step in your Bible study journey with the Devoted Scripture Journal. This daily guide will help you read the Bible consistently, engage with God through His Word, and record your encounters with Him.

Learn more at jazminnfrank.com/books

Also Available

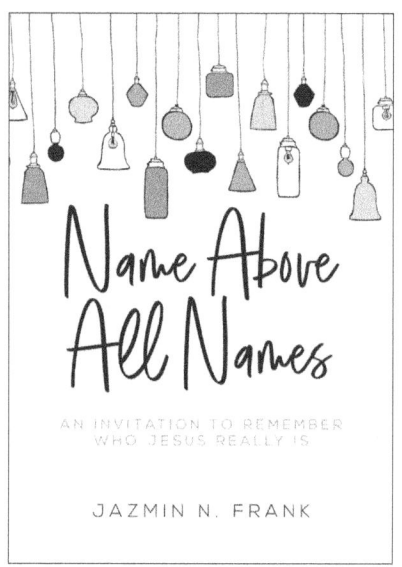

It's time to remember who Jesus really is. Spend the next thirty-one days studying the names of Jesus through the Gospel of John. Not only will you learn more about who Jesus is, but you'll also be reminded of who you are in Him.

Waiting seasons are hard, but they don't have to keep us at a distance from God. In this forty day study, you will come face to face with the God who is with you in the waiting. You'll learn how to draw near to God in seasons of waiting as you spend time studying the stories of people in Scripture who waited.

About the Author

Jazmin N. Frank is an author, teacher, and speaker on all things Bible. With a focus on building relationship with God, Jazmin equips and encourages ordinary people to love God, love His story, and live devoted. She is the author of *In the Waiting* and *Name Above All Names*. Jazmin loves creating Bible studies that help people dive deep into Scripture, while also teaching Bible study skills. Learn more and connect with Jazmin online @jazminnfrank or on her website jazminnfrank.com.

Notes

1. ESV Study Bible: English Standard Version. Crossway, 2008 (see note on Psalm 1:2).

2. Barton, Ruth Haley. Sacred Rhythms: Arranging Our Lives for Spiritual Transformation. InterVarsity Press, 2006.

3. ESV Study Bible: English Standard Version. Crossway, 2008 (see note on Exodus 4:21).

4. "Video: Overview: Exodus 1-18: BibleProject™." BibleProject, 2016, bibleproject.com/videos/exodus-1-18/.

5. ESV Study Bible: English Standard Version. Crossway, 2008 (see note on Exodus 17:2).

6. "Consecrate." Merriam-Webster.com Dictionary, Merriam-Webster, https://www.merriam-webster.com/dictionary/consecrate. Accessed 13 Nov. 2020.

7. "Resistance to Anxiety." Sabbath as Resistance: Saying No to the Culture of Now, by Walter Brueggemann, Westminster John Knox Press, 2017, pp. 21-33.

8. "H5650 - `ebed - Strong's Hebrew Lexicon (CSB)." Blue Letter Bible. Web. 9 Dec, 2020. https://www.blueletterbible.org//lang/lexicon/lexicon.cfm?Strongs=H5650&t=CSB.

9. Junker, Stephanie. Sabbath Movement Suggestions Chart, 2020.

www.ingramcontent.com/pod-product-compliance
Lightning Source LLC
Chambersburg PA
CBHW081507080526
44589CB00017B/2673